With the name of Allah, the All-Merciful, the Most-Merciful

Road of the Shepherds

Abu Muhammad, Qasim ibn Inayat Ali

British Library Cataloguing in Publication Data
A catalogue record of the book is available from the British Library.

Written by; Abu Muhammad, Qasim ibn Inayat Ali

Illustrated by; Ishaq Aamir Chowdhury and Masud Ameen

Edited by; Sheikh Ridwan Kajee, Sheikh Suleman Mall and Bint Inayat

Front Cover Design by; 'We, the People co.'

Published and Distributed by;
Jamiatul Ilm wal Huda
30 Moss Street
Blackburn
Lancashire
United Kingdom

Tel: 01254 673105
Web: www.jamiah.co.uk
E-mail: info@jamiah.co.uk

Also available from:
Quwwatul Islam Masjid
Email: info@quwwatulislam.org.uk

ISBN: 978-0-9556973-6-4

Printed by: Imak Ofset, Turkey

I set off on a journey to recognise my Lord.
I hoped his friendship would be my reward.
Little did I know when I took my first stride,
My Lord was already standing by my side.

- Abu Muhammad, Qasim ibn Inayat Ali -

وَكُلًّا نَقُصُّ عَلَيْكَ مِنْ أَنْبَاءِ الرُّسُلِ مَا نُثَبِّتُ بِهِ فُؤَادَكَ ۚ وَجَاءَكَ فِي هَٰذِهِ الْحَقُّ وَمَوْعِظَةٌ

وَذِكْرَىٰ لِلْمُؤْمِنِينَ

"And We narrate to you all such stories from the events of the messengers as We strengthen your heart therewith. And in these (stories) there has come to you the truth, a good counsel and a reminder to those who believe."

- Qur'an 11:120 -

عَنْ أَبِي هُرَيْرَةَ رضى الله عنه عَنِ النَّبِيِّ صلى الله عليه وسلم قَالَ مَا بَعَثَ اللَّهُ نَبِيًّا إِلاَّ رَعَى الْغَنَمَ فَقَالَ أَصْحَابُهُ وَأَنْتَ فَقَالَ نَعَمْ كُنْتُ أَرْعَاهَا عَلَى قَرَارِيطَ لأَهْلِ مَكَّةَ

It has been narrated from Abu Hurayrah (may Allah be pleased with him) that the Messenger (Allah's peace and salutations be upon him) said, "Allah did not send any messenger except that he used to herd sheep." So the companions enquired, "And you?" Thus the Messenger (Allah's peace and salutations be upon him) replied, "Yes, I used to herd them for the people of Makkah in lieu of qarareet (money)."

- *Narrated by Imam Bukhari (may Allah have mercy upon him)* -

What day is a day upon which the sun does not shine?
What man is a man who is not enlightened with imaan?

How dark is the night which does not bring the moon to guide?
How dark is the road of the traveller who does not choose Rasulullah ﷺ as his guide.

How frightening is the night sky which is not beautified with stars?
How frightening is the man who is not beautified with good character.

How barren is that land which bears no fruit?
How barren is that life in which the land of the hereafter is not ploughed?

What sea is a sea that has not a drop of water?
What eye is an eye that has not shed a tear out of fear for Allah?

What clouds are clouds that bear no rain?
What moments are those in which the mercy of Allah we do not gain?

What trees are trees that have no roots?
What heart is a heart that has no faith?

What mountains are mountains that have no rocks?
What faith is faith that has no firmness?

What river is a river which does not flow?
What belief is belief that to make others believe man does not go?

How desolate is the heart which is not inhabited by Allah's love?

How blind are the eyes which do not see Allah's greatness?

How clouded is the mind which does not recognise Allah's oneness?

How paralysed is the body which does not bow to Allah's commands tirelessly?

How withered is the tongue which does not remember Allah continuously?

How deaf are the ears which do not listen to Allah's words attentively?

How futile is that word spoken which does not increase one's love for Allah?

How frivolous is that word heard that does not bring one closer to Allah?

Contents

Acknowledgements

Rasulullah ﷺ said, "He who does not thank the people has not truly thanked Allah."

Therefore, I would like to express my sincerest gratitude to my beloved mother and father, to my dearest wife and my cherished siblings, Anas, Faizal, Umm Adam and Bint Inayat for their moral support and assistance during the years I took to write this book.

I secondly thank Sheikh Ridwan Kajee, Sheikh Suleman Mall and my sister for reading through the manuscript and highlighting areas which required changes. Also to Ishaq Aamir Chowdhury and Masud Ameen, who made a concerted effort to do the illustrations in a very short timeframe, despite their numerous commitments.

I gratefully acknowledge the earnest advice, input, help and ideas given to me by Mufti Minhaj Barwat, Sheikh Muawiyah ibn Mufti Abdus Samad, Sheikh Zubair Ahmed, Sheikh Khalid Ibrahim, Hafiz Yasir Gotly, Hafiz Asim Galya, Sheikh Yusuf ibn Bashir, Mufti Abid Molvi, Sheikh Ikram Khanjra, Safwan Khanjra, and Zaid Patel.

I thank all of my teachers at Jamiatul Ilm Wal Huda (Blackburn, England), Madrassah Arabia Islamiyyah (Azaadville, South Africa) and Masjid e Tauheedul Islam (Blackburn, England) for the knowledge they passed on to me without which I would not have been able to pen down these rhymes.

And finally I would like to mention Sufyan Mohmed, because he wanted to be cited in this book which contains stories of some of the accepted servants of Allah; hoping that he too can be named with them on the day of Judgement and gain entry into Paradise alongside them.

May Allah accept their efforts, grant them His divine pleasure and make their final abode amongst the messengers, the sideeqeen, the martyrs and the pious.

Author's Foreword

الحمد لله نحمده ونستعينه من يهده الله فلا مضل له ومن يضلل فلا هادي له واشهد ان لا اله الا الله وحده لا

شريك له وان محمدا عبده ورسوله اما بعد

"All praise belongs solely to Allah. We praise Him and seek His assistance only.
Whomsoever He guides none shall ever mislead him, and for whomsoever misguidance He
decrees, none shall ever be able to guide him. I bear witness that there is no deity but Allah
and I bear witness that Muhammad ﷺ is the servant and messenger of Allah."

All praise is for Allah, the Lord of the worlds, who has saved us from the darkness of disbelief and has illuminated our hearts with the light of imaan. Glorified is ar-Rahman who sent the messengers, the best of men, to guide humanity towards the path of righteousness which leads to the pleasure of the Creator. Greatest is ar-Rahim, whose complete and all-encompassing mercy did not leave mankind blind in the depths of darkness, in which they would have been ignorant of the enlightened road to salvation. Majestic is as-Saboor, who gives mankind opportunity after opportunity to turn to Him in repentance despite mankind's persistent disobedience and sinning. Magnanimous is al-Gaffar, who anticipates the moment his servants turn to Him in repentance and eagerly forgives all the sins of the sinners.

May His salutations be on His beloved Rasul ﷺ, who is a mercy to mankind and an exemplary role model who laboured tirelessly throughout his life to ensure each individual from his Ummah can reach man's ultimate goal. He who constantly worried and made concern about how every person can be saved from the flaming fires of Hell and be granted entry into the gardens of eternal bliss. I pray that each of our actions is done solely for the pleasure of Almighty Allah.

I start by praising Allah for the uncountable, immeasurable, infinite blessings He has bestowed upon me even though I have not proved to be worthy of them. I beseech Allah to send peace and salutations upon Rasulullah ﷺ, the mercy to mankind and the perfect teacher, who never left a stone unturned in explaining the deen of Allah to his Ummah.

Since I was a child I have had a passion for reading, it was my greatest source of entertainment. My father would buy me books which I would read with great fervour, but none so much as the books he brought which told the stories of the messengers. I found them to be inspirational and would read them again and again. My copy of the translation of '*Stories of the Messengers*' by Moulana Abul-Hasan Ali an-Nadwi ﷺ was read so frequently that its pages hung from the strings that bound it together.

I loved the stories of the messengers to such an extent that I had an inner desire burning within me. I used to day-dream about this aspiration coming true, to the point where I would imagine how it could happen and even as to where it could happen. I was still young and had only been attending madrasah for a few years, but I had not reached an age where I could fully understand the fundamentals of deen. When I could no longer keep this wish to myself I decided to confide in someone and thus approached my eldest sister one day. I can still distinctly remember I disclosed my ambition to her whilst she was in the kitchen at the sink. I divulged, "When I grow older I want to become a messenger." My sister whipped around and scolded me saying the Messenger Muhammad ﷺ is the last Messenger and no messenger is to come after him. I am eternally grateful to my sister for imparting to me this essential and fundamental belief.

I now pray that as I could not be with the messengers in this world, Allah unites me with them in the hereafter. The Messenger ﷺ said, '*A man will be with whom he loves (in the hereafter)*'. May this book serve as a witness to the love I have for the messengers of Allah and a means of me being enveloped in the mercy of Allah with them on the Day of Resurrection.

I decided to name this book 'The Road of the Shepherds' due to the hadith of Rasulullah ﷺ in which he mentions that every single messenger tended sheep at some point in their lives, as well as the hadith in which Rasulullah ﷺ refers to every individual as a shepherd, each of whom has his own flock for which they are accountable. I also hope this book can serve to be like a shepherd in which the reader can contemplate over the lives of the messengers and take account of their own lives, by which they can be led towards the path of righteousness. Furthermore, I pray it serves as a reminder that each individual is going to be held accountable for every moment of his life in the court of Allah.

I pray to Allah to accept my humble efforts and pray that He makes this book a means of guidance, a source of gaining closeness to Him and a cause of acquiring love for the messengers and their way. And I ask Allah to forgive all of my shortcomings.

اللهم اليك اشكوا ضعف قوتي وقلة حيلتي ...

'O Allah, only to you do I complain of the feebleness of my strength and my lack of resources...'

Abu Muhammad, Qasim ibn Inayat Ali

Introduction

Allah created and fashioned Adam ﷺ, who is the first man and our father, from clay. It is to this soil that we, his progeny, will return and from it we will once again be raised. It is perturbing how man knowing that he was made from clay and that is where he will inevitably return is haughty and proud of himself. If man was to contemplate on the reality of his origins he would come to an understanding that at first he was nothing.

We learn from the Qur'an that Shaytaan refused to bow to Adam ﷺ when Allah commanded him. This was due to the fact that Adam ﷺ was made from clay whereas Shaytaan was made from fire. Shaytaan believed that fire was superior to clay as it rises when it is lit, whereas clay falls when it is dropped. Using this reasoning Shaytaan thought he should not fall prostrate to a being made of clay and he refused to bow. Thus we learn that due to the substance that Shaytaan was made of, i.e. fire, he had the quality of pride in him. So then as men, being made of clay, are we not supposed to have the quality of humbleness within us?

Moreover, if one contemplates on his origins and how Allah describes the beginning of man in the holy Qur'an, he will realise that all the components of man are insignificant and of a low, meaningless disposition. Yet if we reflect on these profound verses of the Qur'an we perceive the greatness of Allah in that He created the noblest of creations from things that have no value to us.

هل اتى على الانسان حين من الدهر لم يكن شيئا مذكورا. انّا خلقنا الانسان من نطفة امشاج نبتليه فجعلنه سميعا بصيرا

"Did a long period of time not come upon man wherein he was nothing, not even mentioned? Verily we created man from a drop of mingled sperm in order to test him, thus we gave him the ability to hear and see."

(Surah al-Insaan, verses 1-2)

From the stories of the messengers, we are able to understand the height of humbleness in them. Even though they are the greatest of personalities, the best of creation and those most beloved to Allah, they never show an iota of pride to those to whom they were sent. Rather, they tolerated and endured with great forbearance all the hardships, which their people meted out upon them. At no point in their lives do we find that they felt more worthy or better than their people. Rasulullah ﷺ mentions in a hadith, *"He who humbles himself for the sake of Allah, then Allah will raise him (in status), and he who is proud, Allah will degrade him."*

People denied the truth of the messengers due to the pride which came with their wealth, position and power. Their pride resulted in their unwillingness to accept the truth. How sad is our state of affairs that after having accepted the truth of the messengers and claiming to believe in them, our actions are contrary to what we believe and they portray the same denial as that of the disbelievers?

We further learn that after Allah had fashioned Adam علیه السلام, He left him in that state for a certain amount of time. He did not immediately give him life. We should take a lesson from this that for Allah to bring something into existence, all He has to say is, "Be", and it is. However Allah did not create Adam علیه السلام in haste, in the same manner that Allah took six days to create the heavens and the earth and that which is between them. Had Allah wished, He could have said *"Be,"* and it would have all been brought into existence.

Haste in matters is not a commendable quality. Moreover the greatest misfortune and grief is upon those people who decide they want to enjoy this life. They hurry and exert all their effort and time in order to enjoy the pleasures of this world and take nothing with them into the eternal life of the hereafter except regret and remorse.

Was the life of those disbelievers who denied the messengers not the same, wherein their purpose in life was to enjoy it and be merry? They were unwilling to give up the pleasures of this world for those of the hereafter. Have we not degraded to that level wherein we have forgotten about the hereafter and run hastily after our share of this world? The sad difference is we have believed in the hereafter whereas those people had denied it. The unfortunate reality of it is that our actions contradict our words.

Man works all his life to build himself an empire in this world. He spends hard laborious years to buy his dream house, which he is never satisfied with and always wants a bigger home. He will always want a bigger garden, better food, more money, greater respect, higher authority and power. Before he knows it he has reached old age and it his time to leave this world. He leaves behind all his worldly efforts only to regret he did not plough the fields of the hereafter.

Take this simple allegorical example. A father gives his two sons a plot of land and some money with which they have to earn their living. They will not be given any more money after this and they need to make use of what is given to them and live off it for the rest of their lives. The first son decides to spend his money on buying exquisite food, luxurious items, expensive clothing and uses it all up on enjoying the varieties of life. Within a year his money is exhausted and his land, overgrown with weeds, is of no use to him.

The second son bought seeds and sowed them in the land. He bought livestock and made them graze in his pastures. He spent time, effort and money on cultivating the land. He only spent a minimal amount of money on the bare necessities and forsook the pleasures, which were enticing and easily available. Within a year his land was lush and green and he had a very profitable harvest. Now he had enough food and goods to maintain a luxurious life and for the remainder of his life he lived off that which his land produced.

If asked which son was wiser, anyone with even the slightest common sense will answer the second one. The money they were initially given represents our time on this earth, we have all been stipulated our amount, which we need to invest as we cannot get anymore. The land they were given are our open, vast and empty fields of Paradise in the hereafter and the seeds which were sown are our deeds. Though at first we cannot see the harvest of that which we have sown, when we go to Paradise we will see the fruits of our efforts.

عَنْ عَبْدِ اللهِ بْنِ مَسْعُودٍ، عَنِ النَّبِيِّ صَلَّى اللهُ عَلَيْهِ وَسَلَّمَ قَالَ: " لَمَّا كَانَ لَيْلَةَ أُسْرِيَ بِي لَقِيتُ إِبْرَاهِيمَ صَلَّى اللهُ عَلَيْهِ وَسَلَّمَ فِي السَّمَاءِ السَّابِعَةِ، فَقَالَ: يَا مُحَمَّدُ، اقْرَأْ عَلَى أُمَّتِكَ السَّلَامَ، وَأَخْبِرْهُمْ أَنَّ الْجَنَّةَ عَذْبٌ مَاؤُهَا، طَيِّبٌ شَرَابُهَا وَأَنَّ فِيهَا قِيعَانًا، وَأَنَّ

غَرْسُ شَجَرِهَا سُبْحَانَ اللَّهِ، وَالْحَمْدُ لِلَّهِ، وَلَا إِلَهَ إِلَّا اللَّهُ، وَاللَّهُ أَكْبَرُ

Abdullah ibn Masood ﷺ narrates from the Messenger ﷺ, that he said, "On the night in which I was taken for the night journey (to the heavens), I met Ibrahim ﷺ in the seventh sky. Ibrahim ﷺ said "O Muhammad, send salutations upon your nation, and inform them that the water of Paradise is sweet, its wine is delicious, and verily in it is a land without vegetation, and the planting of its trees are (to say) 'Subhana-Allah' and 'Alhamdu-lillah' and 'La-ilaha-illal-lah' and 'Allahu-akbar'."

(Musnad Bazzar)

To earn the pleasures of this life can be painstakingly difficult. On the other hand, though great sacrifices are required to attain Paradise, some of its blessings can be acquired through simple deeds. Ibrahim ﷺ told the Messenger of Allah ﷺ to inform us that Paradise is an empty land and it is up to us to build our empire and our eternal abode through our deeds. There are simple ways of building palaces and gardens in paradise as has been enumerated in the following two ahaadith.

إِنَّ نَبِيَّ اللَّهِ صَلَّى الله عَلَيْهِ وَسَلَّم قَالَ:مَنْ قَرَأَ قُلْ هُوَ اللَّهُ أَحَدٌ عَشَرَ مَرَّاتٍ، بُنِيَ لَهُ بِهَا قَصْرٌ فِي الْجَنَّةِ، وَمَنْ قَرَأَهَا عِشْرِينَ مَرَّةً، بُنِيَ لَهُ بِهَا قَصْرَانِ فِي الْجَنَّةِ، وَمَنْ قَرَأَهَا ثَلَاثِينَ مَرَّةً، بُنِيَ لَهُ بِهَا ثَلَاثَةُ قُصُورٍ فِي الْجَنَّةِ

The Messenger of Allah ﷺ said, "Whoever prays 'Qul huww-Allahu ahad' (i.e. Surah Ikhlaas) ten times a palace is built for him in Paradise because of it. And whosoever prays it twenty times, two palaces are built for him in Paradise because of it. And whosoever prays it thirty times three palaces are built in Paradise for him because of it."

(Sunnan ad-Darmiy)

عَنْ أَبِي هُرَيْرَةَ، أَنَّ رَسُولَ اللَّهِ . صلى الله عليه وسلم. مَرَّ بِهِ وَهُوَ يَغْرِسُ غَرْسًا فَقَالَ " يَا أَبَا هُرَيْرَةَ مَا الَّذِي تَغْرِسُ " . قُلْتُ غِرَاسًا لِي . قَالَ " أَلاَ أَدُلُّكَ عَلَى غِرَاسٍ خَيْرٍ لَكَ مِنْ هَذَا " . قَالَ بَلَى يَا رَسُولَ اللَّهِ . قَالَ " قُلْ سُبْحَانَ اللَّهِ وَالْحَمْدُ لِلَّهِ وَلاَ إِلَهَ إِلاَّ اللَّهُ وَاللَّهُ أَكْبَرُ يُغْرَسُ لَكَ بِكُلِّ وَاحِدَةٍ شَجَرَةٌ فِي الْجَنَّةِ " .

Abu Hurayrah ﷺ narrates that verily the Messenger of Allah ﷺ passed by him whilst he was planting seedlings. The Messenger ﷺ said, "O Abu Hurayrah, what is it that you are planting?" I replied, "Seedlings for me." The Messenger ﷺ said, "Should I not direct you

towards plants that are better for you than this?" I replied, "Surely, O Messenger of Allah."
The Messenger ﷺ said, "Say 'Subhana-Allah' and 'Alhamdu-lillah' and 'La-ilaha-illal-lah'
and 'Allahu-akbar', a tree will be planted for you in Paradise for each one (of these
phrases)."

(Sunan ibn Majah)

The world is a farm of the hereafter. Ibrahim ﷺ informed Rasulullah ﷺ to tell us that our Paradise is a vast open plain land. It is up to us to cultivate it in this world and enjoy its eternal pleasures in the hereafter. There are numerous verses of the Qur'an and a vast number of ahaadith which accentuate the beauty and allure of Paradise. Suffice it to say, it is that which no eye has seen, no ear has heard and that which cannot be comprehended by the heart of man.

It has been said that there were four kings who ruled the entire world. Two were believers and two were disbelievers. The believers were Sulayman ﷺ and Zhul Qarnayn and the disbelievers were Bukhtanasr and Namrud.

Man at first desires wealth. When he has accumulated wealth to the highest degree he aims to gain prestige amongst the people. When he feels he has accomplished this he wants authority. When he has expanded his authority over the people he craves for power, after which he yearns for kingship. Namrud had gained kingship to the highest degree as he ruled the known world. So he had no further worldly means of progression. Thus he claimed divinity and challenged the King of kings.

With regards to the manner in which Allah destroyed Namrud, it is mentioned that he challenged Allah against his army and questioned Ibrahim ﷺ where the army of his Lord was, to which Ibrahim ﷺ replied, *"Soon you will see the doing of His weakest army."*

Allah sent upon them a cloud of mosquitoes which ate them and their animals to such an extent that their bones were gleaming white. However it was destined for Namrud to survive. A mosquito entered through his nose and went into his brain. It attacked him internally and drank the blood from his brain.

To find relief from the pain of the mosquito he would tell someone to hit his head with force. When he was hit on the head the mosquito would desist from attacking his brain, but then his head would hurt from the severe beatings. Like this he suffered greatly for a very long time, when the internal pain would become too hard to bear he would order someone to beat his head until the external pain was too much to bear.

Finally Namrud found no alternative and called for a servant. "*Strike my head!*" he ordered his servant.

The servant drew his sword and split Namrud's head in two. Unfortunately the mosquito was also struck by the sword and lost one of its wings. It cried out, "*O my Lord, I entered in compliance to your command, and now my wing has broken.*"

Allah replied, "*Do you wish for recompense or do you desire your wing back?*"

The mosquito asked, "*What is the recompense?*"

Allah answered, "*The equivalent of the world since I created it until I destroy it.*"

The mosquito replied, "*I do not desire that, I want my wing.*"

Usually a man who conquers and kills the king of a land becomes the owner of the previous king's kingdom. The mosquito too could have asked for the kingdom but only asked for its wing to be repaired. We must take heed from this, that the ruler of the world, who was considered the greatest man alive and who himself thought he was a god was killed by a tiny and weak mosquito. Moreover, this mosquito had the sense to realise that this world was only temporary and therefore only asked Allah for its needs rather than its desires.

عَنْ سَهْلِ بْنِ سَعْدٍ، قَالَ: قَالَ رَسُولُ اللهِ صَلَّى اللهُ عَلَيْهِ وَسَلَّمَ: لَوْ كَانَتِ الدُّنْيَا تَعْدِلُ عِنْدَ اللهِ جَنَاحَ بَعُوضَةٍ مَا سَقَى كَافِرًا مِنْهَا شَرْبَةَ مَاءٍ.

Sahl bin Sa'd ﷺ narrates that the Messenger of Allah ﷺ said, "If to the Allah the value of the world was equal to that of the wing of a mosquito he would not give a disbeliever from it (i.e. the world) one sip of water to drink."

(Sunan at-Tirmizhi)

The mosquito, a creation which is considered as insignificant and weak, realised that the value of the world was worthless if it meant it had to lose its wing. What use is this life going to be, if it meant having to sacrifice its wing? Why then cannot man, who is the best of creations and has been honoured with intelligence, not realise that the value of the world is worthless if it means having to lose the eternal pleasures of the hereafter? What use is this fleeting world going to be to us if we have to sacrifice Paradise for it? What use is this temporary world going to be to us if we are going to have to endure the unbearable torments of Hell because of it?

The fulfilment of your needs will satiate you whereas to fulfil your desires will only make you hungry for more. Allah gave Namrud a kingdom the likes of which no one had received before, and Namrud claimed divinity which no one had done before. Initially he had waged war against the kings of the world but now he waged war against the King of kings, the King of the heavens and the earth, by claiming divinity. Observe his final end, how could he have stood against Allah when he was annihilated by a mere mosquito.

Rather than chasing this world and its temporary pleasures, its wealth, prestige, honour, governance and status we need to truly acknowledge that whatever we are to earn in this world has already been stipulated for us even before we were born. The world was created for us, and we are created for the hereafter. So rather than foolishly trying to attain what is already ours, we need to make an effort for that which needs to be earned.

Once, King Namrud summoned Ibrahim ﷺ to his court, in order to question him regarding his beliefs. Namrud claimed to be a god and he feared that Ibrahim's ﷺ faith would put his divinity to question. The dialogue which ensued between the two of them is mentioned in the Holy Qur'an:

'Have you not reflected upon the one to whom Allah gave a kingdom who argued

with Ibrahim ﷺ regarding his Lord. When Ibrahim ﷺ said, "My Lord is He who gives life and causes death." He replied, "I too give life and cause death.'

Namrud then called for two men, he killed one and spared the other. He attempted to prove that he also had power over life and death. When Ibrahim ﷺrealised that this reasoning would not work against the clouded mind of Namrud he resorted to reasoning with a power which Namrud could not claim.

'Ibrahim ﷺ said, "Verily Allah causes the sun to rise from the east, you then cause it to rise from the west." Thus the one who disbelieved was confounded.'

Here the question could be posed that how Namrud was foolish to claim that he had power over life and death, similarly, why didn't he claim that he was the one who caused the sun to rise from the east? Why did he not ask Ibrahim ﷺ to tell his Lord to cause it to rise from the west instead? The reason for this is that even though he claimed to be a god, he knew within his heart that Allah is the one true Lord of the heavens and the earth. He truly believed that if he was to put the same challenge forward to Ibrahim ﷺ then Allah would have changed the whole system of the world by causing the sun to rise from the west, due to which he would have lost his claim to divinity.

Ponder over the conviction of Namrud. A man who claimed to be god had so much conviction in Allah that he was convinced if he challenged Allah, then Allah would have made the sun rise from the west. We face obstacles in our lives in which science, experience and knowledge tells us that to overcome such an obstacle is impossible. We need to have firm faith that Allah is capable of all things. He has power over everything. Allah can make the extraordinary happen. How miracles used to happen at the hands of the messengers, if we were to make an effort on our imaan, we too will see miracles happening in our everyday lives.

Contemplate on the faith of those magicians of Firown who had been enlightened with imaan. Prior to affirming their faith in Allah, they had been summoned to compete against Moosa ﷺ in a magic contest because Firown considered the miracles of Moosa ﷺ as nothing but magic tricks. The magicians were desirous of the wealth and luxuries of the temporary world, so they asked Firown, *"Will we be rewarded if we gain the upper-hand?"*

Firown replied, *"Yes, and indeed you will then be amongst those who are near (to me)."* Firown considered himself as a god who had palaces under which rivers flowed. He did not stipulate a certain countable reward for the magicians. Rather he promised them something they deemed much greater than any material reward. If the magicians were made from amongst those who were near and dear to Firown, then he would give them whatever they desired whenever they desired it.

When the contest began the magicians threw their ropes and sticks which began moving like snakes. They were ecstatic and believed that they had outdone Moosa ﷺ. When Moosa ﷺ threw his staff it transformed into a huge snake which devoured the magic of the magicians. The magicians were awestruck and immediately fell into prostration to Allah, having recognised that what Moosa ﷺ had done was not magic. The proclaimed loudly, *"We have believed in the Lord of the Worlds, the Lord of Moosa and Haroon."*

Firown was furious. The truth of Moosa ﷺ and Haroon's ﷺ apostleship and message had been made clear to all. To undermine the magicians and their faith he bellowed, *"You believed in Moosa before I gave you permission? He is indeed your leader who taught you magic, but soon you will know. I will surely cut off your hands and your feet from opposite sides and I will hang you on the trunks of palm trees. Then you will know which of us is more severe in torment and ever-lasting."*

Firown had threatened to sever either the right hand and left foot or the left hand and right foot of each magician and then have them crucified, whilst they were suffering from this unbearable pain. However the magicians had been blessed with true faith, they had been enlightened with it mere moments before. Such faith cannot be swayed by even the strongest winds of disbelief. They boldly answered back to Firown, *"We will never give you preference over that which has come to us of clear proofs and over that Being who has created us. So decree whatever you are to decree, you can only decree for this worldly life."*

The magicians, who had minutes before been promised the greatest reward that Firown could give, had now been threatened with the severest punishment that Firown could mete out. The strength of their imaan did not incline them towards the promised riches, nor did it allow them to feel any fear for the pain and agonies they would have to endure.

Now reflect upon our imaan. Many of us have been blessed with faith from birth. We have had more time, opportunities and chances to strengthen our imaan. Taking this into account how many of us forsake our obligatory duties to Allah and His creation in trying to attain our allotted portion of this world? How many of us would tremble or forsake Islam if we were threatened with death?

Sulayman ﷺ once prayed to Allah for a kingdom the likes of which had not been given to anyone before him, nor would be surpassed by anyone after him. Allah granted him this kingdom. He was able to understand the language of animals. He was given control over the wind, which would carry his throne allowing him to travel a journey of a couple of months in mere hours. The wind would also carry voices to his ear allowing him to hear words spoken a long distance away.

He was given command over the jinn. They used to construct architectural masterpieces, strong forts, palaces and beautiful cities for him. They would make statues of immense beauty and bowls as large as ponds for people to eat from. They would build large firm pots for cooking. Some would dive deep into the oceans to mine for precious jewels.

It has been narrated that once Sulayman ﷺ was travelling upon his throne with his grandeur and dignity. He happened to pass by a man from Banu Isra'eel. The man was overwhelmed by the power and kingdom which had been granted to Sulayman ﷺ. He exclaimed, *"Subhana-Allah! (Glory be to Allah) Indeed the family of Dawood has been gifted with a unique kingdom!"*

The wind carried the voice of the man and placed it at the ear of Sulayman ﷺ. He ordered for the man to be brought in his presence. He enquired from him why he had exclaimed what he had uttered. He then said to him, *"The reward for one 'Subhana-Allah' on the day of judgement shall be far greater than whatever the family of Dawood has been given in this earthly life."*

Deliberate over the similarity of Sulayman's ﷺ kingdom with today's technology. The travelling on the wind can be likened to aeroplanes, the wind carrying voices to mobile communication, the architectural masterpieces to the large cities with skyscrapers, large pots for cooking to industrial factories and the diving jinn to submarines. If we were given these today we would control the land, the sea and the air. Who can truly say they would give up all of this for one 'Subhana-Allah'? We have become such that we are willingly disobeying the acts Allah has made incumbent upon us for the pennies of this world. Messengers were sent to guide us and assist us in realising that the wealth and power of this world will definitely come to an end, but the rewards of good deeds will last forever.

We need to make an effort on our imaan such that one 'Subhana-Allah' becomes more precious to us than all the riches and wealth of this world.

I pray that by reading the stories of the messengers, we are reminded of our true purpose in life. And I hope that these narratives serve as a means of strengthening our faith. We should further realise from these stories that Allah is not bound to use means. Allah does with means, without means and against means to help his servants. If we were to make an effort on our imaan then we will also experience similar miracles which the messengers and their companions experienced.

Life is an opportunity; only once does it come.
It flies by so many and is only seized by some.

خلق الله تعلى آدم من طين   وتركه في هيئته حتى حين

يا أَسفاه علي الناس المتكبرين   وعلى الذين في أمورهم معجلين

"Allah Ta'ala created Adam ﷺ from clay,
And left him in that state for a while,
Misfortune upon those people who are proud,
And upon those who are hasty in their matters."

- Abu Muhammad, Qasim ibn Inayat Ali -

Adam

The Creation of Man

To create Adam ﷺ, Allah sent Jibra'eel ﷺ to the earth to get some clay.

"I seek Allah's refuge from your decreasing or disfiguring me," the earth did say.

Upon hearing this, Jibra'eel ﷺ returned to Allah without taking one bit,

And said, *"My Lord, the land sought refuge in you, so I granted it."*

Allah then sent Mika'eel ﷺ; and the same thing did occur.

He returned to Allah; from the earth, clay he did not procure.

Allah then sent the Angel of Death ﷺ; Allah's refuge was sought by the land.

He replied, *"I also seek Allah's refuge that I return without fulfilling His command."*

From different lands, different types of dust did he take.

The children of Adam ﷺ, from different compositions of clay Allah did make.

White, red, black and yellow people make up mankind.

In life good and evil, ease and sorrow and everything between them we find.

"I am going to place a vicegerent upon the earth," to the angels, Allah said.

They replied, *"Will You place those who will cause mischief, and blood, they will shed?"*

The angels told Allah that they praise Him and only Him do they glorify.

"I know that which you do not know," was Allah's reply.

Allah created the first man from clay,

And left him in this state for many a day.

Allah then breathed in him soul and life.

From his lower rib Allah created his wife.

Allah blew His spirit into Adam ﷺ; he sneezed when it reached his head.

"All praise belongs to Allah," are the words Adam ﷺ said.

Allah replied, *"Your Lord has had mercy upon you"*; with these words he was greeted.

Now whenever a Muslim sneezes these same words are repeated.

When the spirit reached his eyes, the fruits of Paradise came into sight.

When it reached his stomach, for food he gained an appetite.

Before the spirit reached his legs, he reached out so the fruit he could taste.

Allah therefore says, *"Man is created from haste."*

Man's Enemy

Towards Adam ﷺ, Allah told the angels and Iblees to bow

Shaytaan rejected, and retorted with 'How?'

Shaytaan reasoned, 'Clay falls, whilst fire does rise.'

He questioned the authority of Allah, the all-Wise.

From then on, for man, he was an enemy sworn.

He promised he would not go to hell alone.

In Shaytaan there was arrogance and pride.

He swore that mankind he would misguide.

Allah had taught Adam ﷺ the names of everything.

These things in front of the angels, He did then bring.

The names of these things, from the angels were sought.

They exclaimed, *"We have no knowledge except that which You have taught."*

Towards Adam ﷺ, the same question was turned.

Adam ﷺ informed the angels of the things which he had learned.

Allah said, *"Did I not tell you, the unseen in the heaven and earth I know,*

And I know what you reveal, and that which you do not show." [1]

To learn how to greet, to a group of angels, Adam ﷺ was sent.

"Peace be upon you," Adam ﷺ greeted, when to the angels he went.

"And peace be upon you and the mercy and blessings of Allah," was their reply. [2]

"O Adam, this is your greeting, and that of your offspring," said Allah, most-High.

Life in Paradise

Adam ﷺ was lonely; he wandered around Paradise alone.

Whilst he slept, from his rib his wife was grown.

He found her by his side when he awoke.

About the reason for her creation they spoke. [3]

In Paradise, Adam ﷺ and Hawwa ﷺ lived in ease.

Allah told husband and wife to do as they please.

However, to them both, one condition was made,

To eat from one certain tree, Allah forbade.

The devil tempted them to eat from that tree.

He told them they would be granted immortality.

Adam ﷺ and his wife were fooled by his lure.

They were made to believe that it was death's cure.

And from the forbidden tree they ate,

But blame them not, for it was fate.[4]

They became uncovered when they ate from the tree.

They began covering themselves with leaves, quickly.

Paradise they were all commanded to leave.

Over their wrongdoing, they began to grieve.

For their mistake, upon the earth they were cast.

Adam 🕮 and Hawwa 🕮 regretted their deed of the past.

Life on Earth

'O Lord, we have wronged,' they did cry and plea,

They cried for Allah's forgiveness and mercy.

For days on end they surely did mourn,

Until the way to forgiveness, by Allah was shown.

Upon the earth, for hundreds of years Adam ﷺ did live.

How to live their lives, to his children, advice he did give.

He told them, regarding Shaytaan, they should take care.

Of his tricks and misguidance, they should beware.

Adam's ﷺ Death

Adam ﷺ had fallen ill; he was on his death bed.

"I crave for the fruits of Paradise," he said.

To search for the fruits of Paradise, his children did go.

Whilst searching for the fruits, a group of angels they saw.

"Where are you going? What are you searching for?" the angels did enquire.

They replied, *"Our father is ill, the fruits of Paradise he does desire."*

"Return to your father, he is about to die," the angels said.

Towards Adam ﷺ, his children and the angels did head.

Hawwa ﵂ recognised the angels; to Adam ﷺ she did cling.

She realised that, from her, Adam ﷺ was now departing.

Adam ﷺ had lived for nine hundred and sixty years.

But Hawwa ﵂ did not want to depart from this husband of hers.

Adam ﷺ said to Hawwa ﵂, his beloved wife, *"Leave me,*

I was born before you, leave me with the angels of the Lord Almighty."

The angels took out his soul, after which a bath they gave.

They then shrouded him and buried him in his grave.

It is the height of foolishness of the foolish one to question the wisdom of the wise.

The First Murder

Habil was Qabil's brother,

Adam ﷺ their father, Hawwa ﷺ their mother.

A twin sister they both had.

One day Qabil became mad.

Qabil was to marry the sister of Habil.

And Habil was to marry the sister of Qabil.

The twin sister of Qabil, prettier was she.

To this arrangement, Qabil did not agree.[5]

Between brothers, to avoid a feud and discord,

They were ordered to make a sacrifice to their Lord.

Whoever's sacrifice Allah would accept and take,

According to that a decision they would make.

Habil picked out the best sheep from his flock,

Whereas Qabil took the worst of his harvest stock.

To accept one of them from heaven a fire came.

The sacrifice of Habil was consumed by the flame.[6]

Qabil became infuriated, and threatened, *"I will surely kill you."*

Habil replied, *"In retaliation, there's nothing I will do."*

Thinking it was fair-seeming he followed his whim,

Qabil was convinced by his nafs to kill him.

Qabil murdered his brother; one of the losers he became,

He regretted his decision; he was now filled with shame.

Qabil didn't know what to do with his brother,

Because, before him, there had died no other.

Allah sent a crow which scratched at the ground.

To bury his brother, the solution was now found.

On seeing the bird he cried, "*Unto me woe,*

Am I not even able to hide the body like this crow."

Though death is inevitable, youth seems eternal.

Sheeth

About Sheeth ﷺ, from the ahaadith we come to know.

He received fifty scrolls, out of the hundred and four.[7]

That he was the son of Adam ﷺ, it has been said,

He took care of mankind's affairs, after his father was dead.

How stars beautify the dark sky so too does good character beautify man who is enshrouded in the darkness of his sins.

Idrees عَلَيْهِ السَّلَام

Idrees ﷺ divided his people into groups of three.

On a religious basis, he split them up accordingly,

Into the subjects, the priests and the kings.

Each of them had responsibility over different things.

Idrees ﷺ was the first man to use the pen.

He travelled to Babylon with his believing men.

Great wisdom and knowledge to him, Allah did give.

Due to Allah's blessings, a longer life he wanted to live. **8**

A longer life he wanted as to him Allah did say,

The reward of the people's deeds, he would get each day.

He told a companion angel about his desire not to die.

So up to the Angel of Death, the two of them did fly.[9]

They met Death's Angel whilst from the heavens he descended.

On the fourth heaven to Idrees's ﷺ request the angel tended.

The angel told the Angel of Death about Idrees' ﷺ request.

But this desire of Idrees ﷺ was going to be an unfulfilled bequest.

To take Idrees's ﷺ life on the fourth heaven, Allah did command.

Death's Angel ﷺ was perturbed as he thought that Idrees ﷺ was on land.

So the Angel of Death obeyed Almighty Allah's call.

On the fourth heaven he took out Idrees's ﷺ soul.[10]

But from this story we must take heed,

We should not believe everything we read.

This is an Isra'eeli narration it has been said,

So we do not believe nor deny what we have read.

Ilm (knowledge) is an everlasting candle which does not benefit unless lit with the flame of aml (acting upon it).

Nooh

The First Idolaters

The people of Nooh ﷺ had gone astray.

They worshipped idols of wood and clay.

The worship of one Allah they forsook,

And bowed to Wadd, Suwa, Yaguth, Nasr and Ya'ooq[11].

The Messenger Nooh ﷺ was sent as a guide.

To call towards Allah, he surely tried.

The oneness of Allah, his nation denied.

At Nooh ﷺ, they would sneer and snide.

Nooh's ﷺ Mission

He made effort for a thousand years and fifty less,[12]

Until he lost hope and made a prayer in distress.

He asked Allah to destroy those who with disbelief were filled.

Allah commanded Nooh ﷺ that an ark he must build.

At the mission of Nooh ﷺ, his nation would mock.

Little did they know they were in for a shock.

They laughed as the ark was so far from the sea.[13]

But Nooh ﷺ carried on building it patiently.

He was commanded to gather two animals of each,

And those few who believed in what he did preach.

Nooh  roamed around the land to find

One male and female animal of each kind.

The Flood

Out of the ovens in the ground, water did burst.

This is where the flood started first.[14]

Allah then commanded the clouds to rain.

The punishment had arrived; then eternal pain.

As the water levels rose higher, the people began to run.

Amongst the disbelievers was Qan'aan, Nooh's son.

Nooh called out, *"O my son, embark with us, with the disbelievers do not be."*

His son replied, *"I will climb a mountain, from the water it will save me."*

Nooh's ﷺ son started to climb up high.[15]

To avoid the flood he surely did try.

He thought, his life, the mountain would save.

He drowned when between them came a wave.[16]

Nooh ﷺ told the believers that forgiveness they should seek.

When the flood ended, the ark settled on Mount Judi's peak.

Everything was destroyed; the disbelievers had perished.

And along with them all that they had cherished.

The sky withheld the rain, the water was swallowed by the ground.

On the flooded land, not a living thing was to be found.

As the second Adam, Nooh ﷺ is also well known,

Because from his progeny, mankind was born.[17]

Fulfilling your needs will satiate you, whilst fulfilling your desires will make you hungrier.

Hud

The Giants of Aad

In Yemen, a place with dunes of sand,

Lived the successors of Nooh ﷺ, on Arabian land.

Almighty Allah sent, to them, the Messenger Hud ﷺ,

Who forbade from evil and called towards good.

The nation of Aad was their name.

Their prosperity was of great fame.

They were giants who had great strength.

Allah had given them lives of long length.

The Invitation of Hud ﷺ

But these people indulged in all types of wrong.

The weak amongst them were oppressed by the strong.

They had abandoned the worship of Allah, the One.

Hud ﷺ was sent to them, as astray they had gone.

From their lifeless deities, for help they would ask.

But idols of wood and stone can never fulfil a task.

Hud ﷺ advised them: 'If from Allah you implore,

He'll give you what you ask for, and so much more.'

They followed the religion of their fathers afore,

Which the nation of Aad refused to let go.

To Hud's ﷺ wise words, Aad was defiant.

"You are possessed, O Hud," accused many a giant.

The Destruction of Aad

They carried on their evil ways; the people of Aad.

They would say that Hud ﷺ has gone mad.

In order for his nation to see the right way,

For a minor punishment, Hud ﷺ did pray.

To them, a famine and drought was sent.

This gave the disbelievers a chance to repent.

But they were stubborn; they remained the same.

For their misfortune, Hud ﷺ they used to blame.

Then a dark cloud came winding along a path.

To the nation of Aad, now came Allah's wrath.

The people started to rejoice; they thought it was rain.

In reality it was their death and then eternal pain.

For eight long days, less one night,

A tornado blew with all its might.

It lifted the people off the ground.

Not a living disbeliever was to be found.

Like dead palm trees, the people fell.

Now they were destined for the fire of hell.

To the believers, protection Allah gave.

For submitting to Him, their lives, He did save.

Don't destroy your shack because of your neighbour's castle.

Salih

The Red Camel

Like their ancestors, the people of Thamud had gone astray.

So Allah sent Salih ﷺ to them; who showed them the right way.

Thamud did not believe, by Allah, Salih ﷺ had been sent.

So they asked him for proof; a miraculous event.

Salih ﷺ had been amongst his people a figure of good hope.

But when he called them to Allah, they were unable to cope.

Before his preaching, Salih ﷺ a chief they were going to make.

Now they told him, their religion, they would not forsake.

The disbelieving people of Thamud asked for a sign.[18]

So Salih ﷺ did as they requested; a miracle divine.

Out of a rock on the mountain, a red she-camel made its way,

It drank all the water from their well every other day.[19]

Though they saw the miracle with their own eyes,

Many still did not believe Salih ﷺ and said he told lies.

They still mocked him and Allah they denied.

For water the camel and the people vied.

Amongst the people of Thamud, the she-camel made its home.

Freely in the land, the miraculous she-camel would roam.

The camel, the people of Thamud, could no longer bear.

The water with the camel, they no longer wanted to share.

Salih ﷺ told them, *"Do not harm her."*

The People of Thamud were going to err.

They were told to let the 'sign of Allah' be, [20]

'Otherwise, Allah will punish you severely.'

They planned to kill her; Qidar and another eight. [21]

For the camel's arrival by the well they did wait.

They hamstrung her; cut her shins and lo!

The camel was killed; she was no more.

Thamud's Punishment

Salih ﷺ, who was eloquent in speech,

Told Thamud that the contract they did breech.

'Soon a severe punishment will come to you.'

The people retorted, *"Bring it if you are true."*

Nine mischief-makers conspired for Salih ﷺ to be killed.

But their plans were against what Allah had willed.

They said, *"If by Salih's family revenge is sought,*

By denying the deed we'll get away with it," they thought. [22]

Their days were short; for numbered they were.

Upon themselves, the wrath of Allah they did incur.

In the early part of the day, as the people dreamed,

All of them perished, when an angel screamed.

Their palatial homes and their lands,

Which they built with their bare hands,

Were of no avail to them, that frightful day.

As dead as tree trunks, in their homes they lay.

Fear that which is to come because of that which has gone.

Ibrahim عَلَيْهِ السَّلَام

Who is my Lord?

The people of Ibrahim ﷺ had abandoned the worship of Allah alone.
Instead they were seen worshipping idols made of wood and stone.
He lived amidst all this indulgence in wrong and sin.
Towards Allah, young Ibrahim ﷺ called his kith and kin.

Ibrahim ﷺ saw a star, when he was covered by the night,
"This is my lord," he said about the star shining bright
But when the star dimmed and faded away,
"I do not love those that set," he did say.

Then he sighted the bright rising moon at night,
'This is my lord,' he called out about the illuminated light,
When the moon set, he said, *"Unless my Lord guides me,*
From the people who have gone astray I will surely be."

When he saw the sun rising, Ibrahim did call,
"This is my lord; this is the greatest (of them all)."
When the sun set, turning towards his people, said he,
"From what you associate with Allah, I am free."[23]

The Broken Idols

The idolaters worshipped that which they had made.

Out of respect, in front of them food and drinks were laid.

His father carved them; idols to the people, he would sell.

"Worship only one Allah," his father he would tell.

He questioned his people, *"What are these statues, to which you are devoted?"*

"We found our fathers worshipping them," the people quoted.

"You and your fathers have been in open error," Ibrahim 🕊️ did say.

They replied, *"Have you brought the truth or are you from those who play?"*

"Your Lord id the Lord of the heavens and the earth," Ibrahim 🕊️ explained.

The people refused to listen; Ibrahim 🕊️ it greatly pained.

"I swear by Allah, I will plan against your idols," Ibrahim did say,

After you have turned your backs, having gone away."

Yet to young Ibrahim's 🕊️ advice, they did not heed.

One day they went away to celebrate; it was their day of eid.

To come along with them, the people did tell.

But Ibrahim 🕊️ replied, *"I am not feeling well."*[24]

From him, the people turned their backs and went away.

He made his way to the idols, to which they used to pray.

The people had laid food for the idols at their feet.

Ibrahim turned to the idols and asked, *"Will you not eat?"*

To the lifeless idols, Ibrahim ﷺ spoke,

"Why are you unable to talk?"

As was expected, he did not receive a reply.

To make the people understand, he would try.

Along with him, to their temple an axe he did take.

All of the idols, except for the biggest one, he did break.

The axe, on the biggest idol, Ibrahim ﷺ placed.

Before the people could return, out of the temple he raced.

When the people came back, the broken idols they saw,

They were lying in pieces; shattered on the floor.

"Who has done this to our idols?" the people did exclaim.

Remembering what Ibrahim had said, upon him they put the blame.

They brought Ibrahim ﷺ forward and asked him whether the idols he broke,

He replied, *"Rather this their big one did it, ask them if they are able to talk".* [25]

The people began to think; the stupidity of worshiping the idols they saw.

Refusing to mend their ways; they said, *"They are unable to talk, very well you know."*

The Fire

For doing this deed, young Ibrahim ﷺ was caught.

For breaking the idols, revenge the people sought.

With rope, they bound his hands and his feet,

Then catapulted him into a fire of intense heat. [26]

Sailing through the air, Ibrahim ﷺ went.

To help him, the angel Jibra'eel ﷺ asked to be sent.

With firm conviction and trust in Allah, said he,

To the angel Jibra'eel ﷺ, *"Allah is enough for me".*

Allah commanded the fire to harm him not.

So it became cool and peaceful instead of hot.

He was in the fire for many days, but he was not burnt.

Yet by the people, a lesson was not learnt.

The Foolish King

King Namrud claimed to be the Lord, most-high.

His claim to divinity, Ibrahim ﷺ surely did deny

He summoned Ibrahim ﷺ to his palace court.

Then questioned him with regards to what he thought.

Ibrahim ﷺ explained that his Lord was eternal; forever he lives,

And to whomsoever he wishes, life and death he gives.

The wretched king replied that life and death he also gave.

He called two men; he killed one whilst the other he did save.

Ibrahim ﷺ told him, *"From the east my Lord causes the sun to rise,*

So make it rise from the west."; Ibrahim's ﷺ question was wise.[27]

To this remark the king had neither a reply, nor any retort.

He was defeated, so he dismissed Ibrahim ﷺ from his court.

Ibrahim ﷺ Leaves Home

Ibrahim's ﷺ father and people with him would strife,

So he left his homeland with his nephew and his wife.

He travelled the land and the oneness of Allah he preached.

He invited the people to Allah, until the land of Sham he reached.

Whilst emigrating from the land, where they used to stay,

They came across the town of a tyrant king, on the way.

Ibrahim ﷺ and his wife, Saarah ؏, the evil king did see.

He was taken aback by Saarah's ؏ beauty.

Towards Saarah ؏, much interest was shown.

The king decided to take her, as his own.

If the king found out she was Ibrahim's ﷺ wife,

To get rid of him, the king would have taken his life.

There were no other Muslims in the land, except him and her.

"Tell him, I am your brother," to Saarah ؏ he did confer. [28]

He had not lied; in Islam, brother and sister they were.

The king called for Saarah ؏ and tried to approach her.

Of her innocence, to Almighty Allah she did plead.

She did ablution and asking for help, prayer she did read.

When the king tried to approach her, he became lame.

Saarah ؏ feared the king would die, and she would get the blame.

To cure the king of this affliction, Saarah ؏ did pray.

When he was cured, again towards Saarah ؏ he made his way.

He became lam again; the king could not get near.

When this happened a third time, the king began to fear.

A grievous mistake the king realised he had made.

With a maiden to serve Saarah ◈, for the mistake he paid.

She returned to Ibrahim ◈, and related everything that did occur.

Her maiden's name was Haajira ◈; to Ibrahim ◈, she gave her.

Ibrahim's ◈ Test

To Haajira ◈, a child, named Isma'eel ◈, was born.

Saarah ◈ wanted a child; in her heart envy was sown.

Haajira ◈ had to leave; she tied a girdle to her back,

So that nobody would be able to follow her track.

They travelled till they reached a valley; arid and bare.

Ibrahim ◈, his wife and his son dismounted there.

Ibrahim ◈ was commanded to leave his son and wife,

In a barren desert land, where there were no signs of life.

Leaving his wife and his son, he began to walk.[29]

When she asked, *"Where to my master?"* he wouldn't talk.

When Haajira ◈ understood it was Allah's decree,

"Allah, who commanded you, is with us," said she.

By leaving them, Allah's command Ibrahim ◈ had obeyed.

When he was out of sight, he lifted his hands and prayed.

He asked Allah to put a yearning, for them, in some people's heart.

Then from the precincts of Allah's house, he did dutifully depart.

An Incident

Wanting to be stronger in faith, Ibrahim ﷺ once said,

"My Lord, show me how you give life to the dead."
He was told by Allah, four birds he should kill,
And put a portion of each of them on a different hill.[30]

The friend of Almighty Allah did as he was told,
Then, taking the name of Allah, the birds he called
Allah put life into the birds that Ibrahim ﷺ slew,
And in haste towards him, the four birds flew.

Though one may turn a blind eye, it does not mean he is blind.

Isma'eel علیه السلام

The Water of Zamzam

Isma'eel ﷺ and his mother had been left on barren land,

In which there was no vegetation; they were surrounded by sand.

Between them, they had a flask of water and a few dates.

Were the mother and son abandoned; left to their fates?

The water and the dates only lasted for a while.

Haajira ﷺ and son were now in tribulation and trial

She frantically searched for water for her beloved son.

Between Mounts Safa and Marwa seven times she did run. [31]

On the seventh round, near her son, someone she saw. [32]

She rushed to her son; by his heel water did flow.

Allah did not abandon them, nor left them to die.

Her son's thirst was quenched; he no longer did cry.

The tribe of Jurhum saw something flying in the sky; a bird.

It was a bird which stays near water[33], so they thought it absurd.

Water there was scarce; towards the bird they made their way.

Finding the water of Zamzam, they asked Haajira ﷺ if they could stay.

Haajira ﷺ gave permission to the people of Jurhum, who came.

She told them, ownership of the water, they could not claim.

Haajira ﷺwanted the company of her neighbours too.

Allah had made the prayer of Ibrahim ﷺ come true.[34]

Ibrahim's ﷺ Sacrifice

When Ibrahim ﷺ returned, he found his son and wife.

His beloved son Isma'eel ﷺ was now a boy full of life.

Allah wanted to test Ibrahim ﷺ, to show who he loved more.

Did he love his Lord or the child his wife Haajira ﷺ bore?

He was sacrificing his son; in a dream, Ibrahim ﷺ did see.

When he told Isma'eel ﷺ, *"Do what Allah has commanded you,"* said he.

To convince them that it was a misconception, the devil did try.

Ibrahim ﷺ threw stones at the devil and was not fooled by his lie.

The devil then tried to deceive the mother and the son.

With stones, the devil they too did shun.[35]

Ibrahim ﷺ took his son; towards the desert they did go.

There he placed his beloved son face down on the floor. [36]

Ibrahim ﷺ tried to sever his son's head,

But the knife would not cut; no blood was shed.

He then heard a voice praising Allah, the most-High.

With a ram, Jibra'eel ﷺ descended from the sky.

Ibrahim ﷺ sacrificed the ram instead of his son.

By his action, the pleasure of Allah he had won.

He had fulfilled the command which in his dream he saw.

After staying for a while, back to Sham he did go. [37]

Ibrahim's ﷺ Visit

Isma'eel ﷺ grew up to become a pious young man.

He got married to a woman from the Jurhum Clan.

Ibrahim ﷺ decided to visit his son one day.

He went to the residence where his son did stay.

Isma'eel ﷺ was out hunting, so he spoke to his wife. [38]

He asked her regarding the condition of her life.

She complained life was hard; there was scarce to eat,

And they only had a diet of bread and meat.

He said, *"Tell your husband to change the threshold of his door,"*

After which Ibrahim ﷺ departed; back to Sham he did go.

When Isma'eel ﷺ returned and heard what his father had said,

He divorced his wife and another woman of Jurhum he wed.

Ibrahim ﷺ decided to go to see his son once more.

He was told his son was hunting, when he knocked on his door.

He asked his wife regarding the condition of the life they led.

She replied it was pleasant and their diet was meat and bread.

When Isma'eel ﷺ returned, she told him an old man had called,

And that he had said, *"The threshold of your door you should hold."*

The old man was her husband's father, she then came to know,

And she was the threshold of Isma'eel's ﷺ door.

His son, once again, Ibrahim ﷺ went to see.

This time Isma'eel ﷺ was sharpening arrows under a tree.

After a long period of time, father and son did meet.

They were overjoyed when each other they did greet.

The Builders of the Ka'bah

Allah commanded Ibrahim ﷺ to build Him a house.

Ibrahim ﷺ returned to Makkah, the home of his second spouse.

Upon the foundations of the first Ka'bah, the building was laid. [39]

Father and son supplicated together whilst the Ka'bah they made.

For completing the Ka'bah, Ibrahim ﷺ required one last stone.

The dimensions and description to Isma'eel ﷺ were shown,

A stone of that description, in the mountains, Isma'eel ﷺ sought.

A brilliant white stone, from the heavens, Jibra'eel ﷺ brought.[40]

When they couldn't reach the top, on a stone Ibrahim ﷺ would stand.

Isma'eel ﷺ would then pass the required materials to his father's hand.[41]

Ibrahim ﷺ was told not to ascribe partners to Allah and to keep His house clean,

And to proclaim the pilgrimage; people would come on foot and camels, lean.[42]

Unity ties U N I together.

Lut

Lut's ﷺ Message

Lut ﷺ was the nephew of Almighty Allah's friend.[43]

Lut ﷺ, to the people of Sodom, Allah did send.

With his uncle, Ibrahim ﷺ, his home he did leave.

In the land of Can'aan, apostleship he did receive.

He was commanded to go to the land of Sodom to preach.

To accept the religion of Ibrahim ﷺ, his people he did beseech.

Lut ﷺ said, to Sodom, *"I am an apostle worthy of all trust."*

His people did not heed, and they had an unnatural lust.

"Obey me, no reward I ask of you for it," he would say.

But attention, to his wise words, his people did not pay.

In public, the disbelieving people were rowdy and rude.

Towards the message of Lut ﷺ, their attitude was crude.

The scandalous people were merciless and without pity.

The followers of Lut ﷺ, they wanted to drive out of the city.

The believers insisted upon staying pure and clean.

His followers had been enriched with Ibrahim's ﷺ deen. [44]

When Lut ﷺ had despaired, for help from Allah he did ask.

Three high ranking angels were sent to fulfil the task.

They came when Lut ﷺ was praying; the guests his daughters did greet,

And the guests, with due courtesy, his daughters did treat.

For the safety of his guests, Lut ﷺ was filled with dread.[45]

News regarding his three handsome guests soon spread.

At his house, the wretched people of Sodom did appear.

This was their final test; now their punishment was near.[46]

The People of Lut ﷺ Perish

The home of Lut ﷺ, his evil people did surround.

Lut ﷺ wished he had support, as no help was to be found.

About his guests being angels, Lut ﷺ still did not know.[47]

The people surrounded his house and tried to break down the door.

Lut ﷺ prayed to Allah to protect his guests, three.

The besiegers were blinded and out of fear did they flee.

The angels put Lut ﷺ at ease when they told him who they were.

Soon the punishment was to come, which the people did incur.

Lut ﷺ with his followers and family, except his wife, fled.[48]

At the break of dawn, the people of Sodom were found dead.

The land of Sodom was overturned after being taken up into the sky,

Whilst stones hailed on those people who did defy.

How stars beautify the dark sky so too does good character beautify man who is enshrouded in the darkness of his sins.

Is'haaq عَلَيْهِ السَّلَام

Ibrahim's عَلَيْهِ السَّلَام Guests

Ibrahim عَلَيْهِ السَّلَام had aged and was now very old.

At his house, three handsome guests called.

These young visitors, Ibrahim عَلَيْهِ السَّلَام knew not.

For the three of them, a roasted calf he got. [49]

But the visitors would not partake of the meat.

To encourage them, Ibrahim عَلَيْهِ السَّلَام started to eat. [50]

When they would not eat, he was filled with dread.

The visitors sensed this; *"Fear not,"* they said.

'We are the angels Jibra'eel ﷺ, Mika'eel ﷺ and Isra'feel,ﷺ' he was told,

And that his wife was to have a child even though, they were old.

Saarah ﷺ clasped her face in surprise, and said, *"Alas for me?"*

To which the angels replied, *"Do you wonder at Allah's decree?"*

Saarah ﷺ was shocked when she heard this news,

The barren wife of Ibrahim ﷺ, these tidings did amuse.

Of the destruction of the people of Lut ﷺ, news they gave.

Only those who believed in Lut ﷺ, Allah would save.

The Glad Tidings

Apostleship to Is'haaq ﷺ, Allah did give.

To gain the pleasure of Allah, a life of piety he did live

And to Is'haaq's ﷺ wife, Ya'qub ﷺ was born,

The tidings had come true which the angels had shown. [51]

The distinguished importance of one does not diminish the virtue of another.

Ya'qub عليه السلام

To the wife of Is'haaq عليه السلام, the Messenger Ya'qub عليه السلام was born.

He is the father of the Jews; as Isra'eel he is also known.

The tidings of his birth were given to his grandfather before. [52]

Through all the trials, Allah tested him with, patience he did show.

Patience makes the life sweeter, for moments plucked before their time will taste bitter.

Yusuf

Yusuf's ﷺ Dream

The story of the Messenger Yusuf ﷺ will now be told.

The 'best of stories', in the holy Qur'an it is called.

It is a moving, heart-rending and touching story of old.

Read on attentively, as the events of his life unfold.

Yusuf ﷺ told his father, Ya'qub ﷺ, *"A dream I did see,*

Eleven starts, the sun and moon were prostrating to me."

His father replied, *"To your brothers, this dream you mustn't relate-*

lest they plot against you and entice you to danger, due to hate." [53]

The Brothers' Scheme

Yusuf ﷺ had ten half-brothers from his father's side,

And one brother from his mother, Ya'qub's ﷺ second bride.

His father's love for him, compared to his brothers, was more,

Due to which, towards Yusuf ﷺ, hatred and malice they did show.

To kill Yusuf ﷺ, his brothers surely did intend,

Or Yusuf ﷺ, to a far-away land they wanted to send.

Finally, in a well, Yusuf ﷺ they decided to leave.

Travellers, in search of water, Yusuf ﷺ they would heave.

So to their father, Ya'qub ﷺ, the brothers went.

To take Yusuf ﷺ to play, they asked for his consent.

He replied, *"Whilst you are unaware, a wolf might eat him, I fear."*

But of their old father's excuse, they would not hear.

They remarked, *"How can a wolf eat him, when a strong group we are?"*

But Ya'qub ﷺ did not like that Yusuf ﷺ, with his brothers, goes far.

Despondently, aged Ya'qub ﷺ gave his beloved son permission to go.

Upon reaching the place, down a well, Yusuf ﷺ they did throw.

The Fake Story

One asked, *"What will we tell our father? A story we need to make?"*

Another replied, *"We'll say a wolf ate him and dye his shirt fake."*

With the blood of a ram, the shirt of Yusuf ﷺ they dyed. [54]

At home they related Yusuf's ﷺ fate, whilst fake tears they all cried.

They wept, *"We left him with our goods, whilst we went to race,* [55]

A wolf ate him;" upon returning, of Yusuf ﷺ there was no trace.

They then presented the blood-stained shirt, which Yusuf ﷺ did wear.

Ya'qub ﷺ knew they lied, as on the shirt there was not a tear. [56]

"For me patience is most befitting," to his sons, Ya'qub ﷺ did say.

Whilst Allah told Yusuf ﷺ, 'of this affair you will inform them one day.' [57]

All alone, in a deep dark well, the treasured son of Ya'qub ﷺ lay.

One day a caravan, travelling to Egypt, passed that way.

Sold!

In need of water, at the well, the caravan stopped.

To draw water, the bucket one of them dropped. [58]

He exclaimed, *"Glad tidings! Here is a boy,"* when Yusuf ﷺ he saw.

As merchandise they hid the boy, who from the well they did draw. [59]

"Who will buy this boy?" in the market place, they called.

To the Minister of Egypt, for a small sum, he was sold.

At his home he told his wife to give Yusuf ﷺ a comfortable stay.

He suggested, *"We shall adopt him as a son, or profit us he may."*

In the Minister's House

Yusuf ﷺ grew into a handsome man; with the minister he did live.

When he reached manhood, to him, wisdom and knowledge Allah did give.

The minister's wife intended evil with him, *"Come, O you,"* said she. [60]

Yusuf ﷺ sought Allah's protection and to the closed door he did flee.

As they raced one another, Yusuf's ﷺ shirt from the back she tore.

Suddenly they found her husband, the minister, upon reaching the door.

She exclaimed, *"The one who intended evil with your family, to prison he should be sent,*

Either that should be his recompense, or a painful torment."[61]

Yusuf ﷺ replied, *"It was she who sought to do evil with me."*

"If his shirt it torn from the front she is true and a liar is he,"

Said someone of the household as witness he bore,

"If it be from the back then she lies and he is true," as the shirt she tore.[62]

The deceiving plots of women, for this incident, the minister did blame.[63]

He said, *"Forget this matter;"* but in the city's palaces it became of fame.

Of the minister's wife's love for her slave, some women of the town spoke.

Upon hearing these comments, she prepared a banquet to end their talk.[64]

The Banquet

The women came for the banquet; for cutting food, they each had a knife.

Whilst cutting their food, *"O Yusuf! Come out before them,"* said the minister's wife.

Distracted by Yusuf's ﷺ beauty, the women cut their hands instead.[65]

"This is not a man, but a noble angel," they said.

"This is the man about whom you did blame me.

I sought to do evil with him, but refused did he.

He will be cast into prison, if my order he doesn't obey.

And will be one disgraced," the minister's wife did say.[66]

Yusuf ﷺ called out, *"My lord! Prison to me is more dear."*

So he was jailed, even though the evidence to the contrary was clear.[67]

With him, into the prison, two young men were sent.

To get their dreams interpreted, to Yusuf ﷺ they went.

Yusuf's ﷺ Imprisonment

To Yusuf ﷺ, one of the companions did thus address,

"I saw myself in a dream, in which wine I did press."

The other narrated, *"I saw myself in a dream carrying bread,*

And there were birds that were eating it from my head."

Yusuf ﷺ said, *"I will inform you of them before your food is brought,*

The interpretations of dreams, from my Lord, I have been taught."

To call them towards Allah, this was a good opportunity he thought.[68]

After which he would give them the information they sought.

Addressing the prisoners; *"O my two fellow prisoners,"* said he,

"Are diverse lords better or Allah the one, the Almighty.

Those which you worship are but names which you and your fathers did name."

Yusuf ﷺ explained then interpreted the dreams, before their food came.

He said, *"As for one of you, for the king he will pour wine,*

The other will be crucified and from his head birds will dine."

He said, to the one who would be saved, *"Mention me to your lord when you go,"*

But Shaytaan made him forget, so Yusuf ﷺ stayed in prison a few years more. [69]

The King's Dream

Seven lean cows devouring seven fat cows, in a dream, the king saw,

And seven green ears of corn, after which seven dry ones did grow.

The king was perplexed, so he told the nobles to explain his dream.

They were unable to interpret it; so a false dream to them it did seem.

Of the king's strange dream, the released wine-bearer heard. [70]

He asked the king to send him forth; to Yusuf ﷺ the dream he conferred.

An interpretation for the king's dream, Yusuf ﷺ did show.

He told the wine-bearer what to do with the crops, which would grow.

Yusuf ﷺ said, *"For seven consecutive years as usual you should sow,*

Except for a little to eat, in its ears, leave the rest which does grow.

Then after those seven years, there will come seven years which will be hard,

It will devour that which you laid in advance, but a little which you did guard."

The wine-bearer was told of an abundant year thereafter; to the king he went.

The king heard the interpretation of his dream; for the interpreter he sent.

Yusuf ﷺ sent a message back to the king, when to release him they came,

"Ask your lord about the women who cut their hands,"; he wanted to clear his name.[71]

So the women who cut their hands by the king were called.

Upon being asked about Yusuf ﷺ, of his innocence they told.

"It was I who sought to do evil," the minister's wife did say.

Now it became clear that, his master, in secret Yusuf ﷺ did not betray.

The Azeez of Egypt

The king spoke to Yusuf ﷺ; *"You are high in rank and trusted,"* said he.

Yusuf ﷺ requested the king, *"Over the storehouses of the land set me."*

Over the storehouses and granaries, Yusuf ﷺ was given command.

For seven years, the people of Egypt tilled and harvested the land.

The people of Egypt would not eat all that which did grow.

Rather, for the forthcoming famine, the food they would store.

Seven fruitful years passed; the famine came, which Yusuf ﷺ had foretold.

People from everywhere began coming to Egypt to buy the food which they sold.

The Famine

In Can'aan lived Yusuf's ﷺ family; there, crops would not grow.

Of an abundance of food in Egypt, they came to know.

For his beloved son, Binyamin, Ya'qub ﷺ did fear.

Not wanting to lose him, he would keep Binyamin near.

When to Egypt the sons of Ya'qub ﷺ went,

Along with them Binyamin was not sent.

In front of him, his brothers, Yusuf ﷺ did see.[72]

They didn't recognise him; Yusuf ﷺ did not reveal his identity.[73]

Yusuf ﷺ was saddened to see that Binyamin, was not there,

He called for food to be brought and gave them their share.

He said, "A brother of yours, from your father, bring to me.

I give full measure and I am the best of hosts do you not see."

He told them no more would be given if they did not bring their brother.

Yusuf ﷺ loved Binyamin dearly because they were born from the same mother.

On Yusuf's ﷺ command, their merchandise in their bags was stowed.

So perhaps they would return to him, after they opened their load.[74]

In Need of More Food

They said to their father, "From the Minister of Egypt we will not receive more.

So send our brother with us, so we get full measure the next time we go."

Ya'qub ﷺ asked, "Should I entrust you, as I entrusted you with his brother before?"[75]

Finding their merchandise, they remarked, "O father, could we desire anymore?"

From the food, they received from Egypt, the family did eat.

As time went on, their stores of food began to deplete.

They had no choice but to return to Egypt to get more.

But they would only receive food if, with them, Binyamin would go.

The King's Bowl

Ya'qub said, "Never will I send him until you promise, by Allah, to bring him back,

Unless you should be surrounded by enemies, which attack.

Do not enter from one gate, but each of you enter from a different gate.

And I cannot avail you at all against Allah's fate."[76]

To Egypt, the sons of Ya'qub ﷺ made their way.

To the advice of their father, attention they did pay.

They all did not enter into Egypt through one gate.

To be given their share of food for Yusuf ﷺ they did wait.

The brothers of Yusuf ﷺ had done as they were told.

When Yusuf ﷺ saw his brother, he quietly took him in his hold.[77]

"Indeed I am your brother," to Binyamin, said he,

"Do not despair over what they used to do to me."

Yusuf ﷺ wished that his brother, with him, would stay.

So he planned a plan; he came up with a way.

His plan to keep him behind, Binyamin he did inform.

This would help him avoid returning home.

His brothers' bags had been loaded; in Binyamin's bag he put the king's bowl.[78]

When they were leaving, *"O caravan, indeed you are thieves,"* an announcer did call.

Whilst being approached, the brother enquired, *"What is it you are missing?"*

To which they replied, *"We have lost the measure of the king."*

The brothers said, *"We did not come to cause corruption nor are we thieves."*

They answered, *"If you should be thieves, what should be the recompense he receives?"*

The sons of Ya'qub ﷺ said, *"In whose bag it is found, he will be given in lieu."*[79]

After searching them from the bag of Binyamin, the bowl they withdrew.

They brothers exclaimed, *"If he steals then a brother of his has stolen before."*

Yusuf ﷺ remained quiet saying, *"Of what you describe, Allah does know."*[80]

They requested him to detain one of them instead and set Binyamin free.

They submitted, *"O minister! An extremely old father has he."*

The protection of Allah, from such a deed, Yusuf ﷺ sought,

That they should take someone other than the person they caught.[81]

When the brothers despaired that he would take none of them in lieu,

They secluded themselves to discuss what they should do.

A Third Son Lost

The eldest brother stayed behind and said, *"To your father you must go,*

Say 'Your son committed theft, we only bear witness to what we saw,

And we could not guard against the unseen,

Ask the caravan and the town to which we have been'."

Another option, the sons of Ya'qub ﷺ could not find,

Other than that the eldest brother should stay behind.

Despondently, towards their home, the brothers turned,

And related the incident, when to Can'aan they returned.

The Reunion

Ya'qub ﷺ said, *"This is a story you yourselves have made."*[82]

But his hope in Allah's mercy did not waver or fade.

He said, *"Maybe Allah will bring them all back to me,*

For indeed full of knowledge and wisdom is He."

From his nine sons, Ya'qub ﷺ turned away,

"How great is my grief for Yusuf," he did say.

Due to his sorrow, Ya'qub's ﷺ eyes became white.

He fell into silence; he had lost his sight.

"By Allah, will you carry on remembering Yusuf," they said,

"Until you reach your last illness or until you are dead."

He replied, "I only complain to Allah of my grief and sorrow,

And I know from Allah that which you do not know."

He instructed his sons to enquire how his missing sons did fare, [83]

And he told them, "Of Allah's mercy, you must not despair."

So the sons of Ya'qub ﷺ went back to Yusuf's ﷺ court.

Help in their distress, from Yusuf ﷺ, they sought.

He said, "Do you know what you did to Yusuf and his brother, whilst you were unaware?"

They asked, "Are you Yusuf?" He was stirred when he heard how they did fare. [84]

He replied, "I am indeed Yusuf and this is my brother," indicating to Binyamin.

They declared, "By Allah, indeed Allah has preferred you above us and we did sin."

Yusuf ﷺ consoled his brothers, "No reproach on you this day.

May Allah forgive you, and He is the most merciful of those who show mercy," he did say.

He gave them his shirt and told them to cast it over his father's face,

Through which he would regain his sight, through Allah's grace.

To bring to him all of their family, he also did tell.

When the caravan departed, their father said, "I sense Yusuf's smell,

If you don't think of me as a man who, due to old age, has weakness of mind."

"By Allah, you are in your old error," the accused the man who'd gone blind.

And when came the one who good news did bear,

He cast over Ya'qub's ﷺ face, the shirt which Yusuf ﷺ did wear.

Ya'qub ﷺ said, upon regaining his eyesight as it was before,

"Did I not say, 'I know from Allah that which you don't know'?"

They begged, "O our father, for our sins forgiveness please implore."

He replied, "Soon, for you, from my Lord forgiveness I will ask for."

So they departed for Egypt and with Yusuf ﷺ they went to live.

To his parents a home with himself Yusuf ﷺ did give.

He raised his parents on a throne and in prostration they all fell.

"This is the fulfilment of my vision of old," to his father he did tell.[85]

He thanked and praised Allah for the position, which he did bestow.

And to die as one submitting to Allah he prayed for.

From the beautiful story of Yusuf ﷺ many lessons one should learn,

Through patience and trust in Allah's mercy, rewards we can earn.

One should always remember Allah whether in difficulty or ease.

And with the pious will be our final abode as Allah we did please.

Revenge is a sweet poison, pleasing to the soul.

Forgiveness is a bitter pill, pleasing to the Lord.

Shu'ayb عَلَيْهِ السَّلَام

Shu'ayb's عليه السلام Message

The people of Madyan had left the worship of their Lord.

They devised ways in which the world they could horde.

When they would sell to others, the buyers they would deceive,

But if they bought then the full amount they made sure to receive.

Allah sent, to them, the 'orator amongst messengers' to teach, [86]

Who had a sweet tone, fluent words and beautiful speech.

Shu'ayb عليه السلام was sent to Madyan and the 'People of the Wood'.

He forbade them from wrong and called them towards good.

Shu'ayb عليه السلام advised them to give full measure, and to pay the full sum,

And worship only Allah or upon them his punishment would come.

His people said they did not understand that which he did speak,

And they considered Shu'ayb عليه السلام from amongst the weak.

The Earthquake

They said, *"If not for your family we would have stoned thee."*

He asked, *"More honoured than Allah to you is my family?"*[87]

Shu'ayb عليه السلام called his people towards Allah again and again,

Until it came to a stage where his call went in vain.[88]

Allah saved Shu'ayb  and those who heeded his warning.

The rest were seized by an earthquake, in the morning.

They were found dead in their homes; lying prostrate.

By refusing to believe in Shu'ayb, they had sealed their fate.

It was as though in that place no one did reside,

The losers were the ones who had denied.

Shu'ayb turned away from those who did disbelieve,

Saying, *"I advised you, so over you how can I grieve?"*

The most inconsiderate one is he who put others in a position he himself would not like to be in.

Ayyoub عَلَيْهِ السَّلَام

The Trials of Ayyoub عَلَيْهِ السَّلَام

Allah had given Ayyoub عَلَيْهِ السَّلَام many servants and wealth,

As well as a lot of children and good health.

Allah tested him by taking these blessings away.[89]

But he was patient and his faith in Allah did not sway.

All of his family, except his wife, were now gone.

But he constantly remembered Allah, the One.

His whole body was afflicted, except his heart and tongue,

With which the praises of Allah he frequently sung.

For many long years this illness of Ayyoub عَلَيْهِ السَّلَام did last.

Still he continued thanking Allah for his blessings; present and past.

To be near Ayyoub عَلَيْهِ السَّلَام, people could no longer stand.

They told him to leave; from the city he was banned.[90]

A Loyal Wife

But there was one person who stood by his side,

Always there to help him, was his faithful bride.

However, she did something which displeased him one day.

"I will lash you a hundred times," Ayyoub عَلَيْهِ السَّلَام did say.[91]

The Reward of Patience

One day someone said that Ayyoub ﷺ must have done something wrong,

Otherwise Allah would not have left him in this state for so long.

To Ayyoub ﷺ this comment someone did relate.

When he heard this accusation, Ayyoub ﷺ fell prostrate.

"Shaytaan has touched me with distress and torment," to his Lord he called.

"Strike with your foot, this is water for a bath and drink," he was told.

After the many years of hardship and loss, which he had patiently endured,

Ayyoub ﷺ was repaid for his patience; with the water he was cured.

The Oath

Allah granted to him his family and much more.

He was given twice as much as he had before.

But he still had to fulfil the oath he had made,

To lash his wife, who had been his loyal aid.

Allah said, "*A bunch of grass, in your hand, you should take,*

And strike with it, your oath you must not break."

Allah saved him from hurting his faithful wife this way.[92]

"*We found him patient, an excellent servant.*" Allah does say.

The Gold Locusts

Whilst Ayyoub ﷺ was bathing, gold locusts started to fall.

In his clothes, Ayyoub ﷺ started to gather them all.

Allah asked, "*Have I not made you independent of that which you see?*"

He replied, "*Surely, but from your blessings there in no independence for me.*"[93]

Victory is not the final result, rather the manner in which you react to victory is. For a man is not praised for his defeat, he is praised for how he dealt with and overcame it.

Yunus ibn Matta عَلَيْهِ السَّلَام

The Departure of Yunus عَلَيْهِ السَّلَام

The people of Nineveh had gone astray.

Yunus عَلَيْهِ السَّلَام called them towards Allah day after day.

They rejected him; his message, they would scorn.

Of the punishment of Allah, his people he did warn.

They would not believe in him, to Yunus عَلَيْهِ السَّلَام, it became clear.

So he left the town; a punishment upon them he did fear.

When Yunus عَلَيْهِ السَّلَام had left, the people saw the punishment draw near,

Repenting, they promised to the true religion they would adhere.

Their faith benefitted them, when they believed.

From the torment of this world they were relieved.

To get away from his people, a ship Yunus عَلَيْهِ السَّلَام did board.

But he had left Nineveh before being commanded by his Lord.[94]

The Storm

Whilst on the ship, there was a great storm.

The people drew lots as was their norm.[95]

They believed that if off the ship a man they threw,

It will cause the raging storm to subdue.

When the lots were drawn, Yunus's  name was drawn out.

Yunus knew this was from Allah, without a doubt.

The waves were furious, the ocean was deep.

Into the ferocious waves, Yunus did leap.

The Repentance of Yunus

Allah commanded a huge fish to swallow him whole.

For many days, in these layers of darkness, Allah he did call.

"There is no god except for You, from all flaws you are free,

Verily I am from the wrong-doers," he said repentantly.

If it was not for his praising of Allah, he would have had to stay

In the stomach of the fish until judgement day.

Allah accepted his prayer and from his grief he was saved.

In the belly of the fish he was no longer enslaved.

Yunus ﷺ had become ill; he was cast onto an open shore.

To cure him, over him a gourd vine, Allah caused to grow.

To a hundred thousand people or more, he was then sent.

They believed in him; so in enjoyment their lives they spent.

Ilm (knowledge) is an everlasting candle which does not benefit unless lit with the flame of aml (acting upon it).

Moosa ﷿ and

Haroon ﷿

The Cruel Ruler

Banu Isra'eel had been living in Egypt for quite long. [96]

It was years after Yusuf ﷿; now they indulged in many a wrong.

They became pleased with the vices of the Egyptian Copt,

Misguided from the true religion, their sins they did adopt.

So they were punished through the Pharaoh's rule,

Who treated them as slaves and was very cruel.

In a dream, Pharaoh saw that to Banu Isra'eel a child was born,

And by this child, his kingdom would be overthrown.

To murder Banu Isra'eel's babies, his soldiers were sent;

His dream from coming true, he wanted to prevent.

Though every single new-born, he intended to kill,

He could not stop that which was Allah's will.

The Birth of Moosa عليه السلام

After Firown's order to kill all male babies, Moosa عليه السلام was born.

To the new-born children of Banu Isra'eel, no mercy was shown.

The family members of Moosa عليه السلام tried to hide him away.

But his mother's fear and worry for him increased each day.

Allah inspired Moosa's عليه السلام mother that Moosa عليه السلام she must feed,

Then put him in the river; to grieve and fear there was no need.

To return her son to her, an oath Allah did take.

And also promised that Moosa عليه السلام a messenger he would make.

Moosa's عليه السلام mother took him to the river; in a box he was placed.

With the current of the water, down the river Moosa عليه السلام raced.

As promised by Allah, the box never sank.

Meanwhile, Firown and his wife, Aasiyah رضى الله عنها were near the river bank.

Moosa عليه السلام was in the box; past Firown's palace it did flow.[97]

He ordered the box to be retrieved; inside a beautiful baby they saw.

Aasiyah رضى الله عنها suggested, *"He could be the coolness of eyes for you and me.*

Do not kill him, our child or of benefit for us he could be."[98]

Moosa ﷺ in the Palace

Moosa's ﷺ sister had followed him as a stranger, but didn't get near.

When Moosa's ﷺ mother heard what happened, for her child she did fear.

By Firown's childless wife, into the palace, Moosa ﷺ was taken.

Allah had ensured that this innocent child was not forsaken.

Then out of hunger baby Moosa ﷺ began to cry.

To feed him and satiate his hunger many women did try.

When Moosa ﷺ would not eat, to feed him, more women were brought.

When Moosa's ﷺ sister saw this, she brought to them the woman they sought.[99]

By ensuring that Moosa ﷺ would drink from no other,

Allah fulfilled His promise and returned Moosa ﷺ to his mother.

Moosa ﷺ, into a young man, the household of Firown did raise.

Allah gave him wisdom and knowledge; qualities worthy of praise.

The Accident

Whilst walking in the city, Moosa ﷺ heard an oppressed Isra'eeli yelp.

He saw a Copt and an Isra'eeli fighting; he went towards them to help.

Moosa ﷺ asked the Copt to stop his abuse; his request the Copt denied.

Out of anger Moosa ﷺ punched him so hard that the Copt died.

He never meant to kill him; *"This if from the devil's doing,"* he did say.

Turning towards Allah, the Merciful, for forgiveness he did pray.

In the city, rumours started when the Copt was found dead.

Until, to Firown's palace, news of the murder had spread.

Firown promised punishment for the person who did the crime.

The next day, Moosa ﷺ saw the same Isra'eeli fighting a second time.

Rebuking him for always quarrelling, towards them he went.

But the Isra'eeli misunderstood what Moosa's ﷺ harsh words meant.[100]

He thought that Moosa ﷺ would strike him when he heard what he did say.

He exclaimed, *"Will you kill me like you killed a man yesterday?"*

Upon hearing this, to Firown's court the Egyptian Copt fled.

And related to them what the quarrelsome Isra'eeli had said.[101]

Warrant for Moosa's Arrest

From the outskirts of the city, came a man from Firown's household.[102]

Of the chiefs' decision to arrest and kill him, Moosa ﷺ was told.

The man advised Moosa ﷺ that from the city he must flee.

He left praying, *"My Lord, from the oppressive folk save me."*

Moosa ﷺ in Madyan

To go to Madyan, who were the descendants of Is'haaq ﷺ, he chose.

He quickly reached Madyan; escaping from his unjust foes.

In Madyan there was a crowd around a well; water they did draw.

Two girls were shunned to the side, Moosa ﷺ saw.

To see the helplessness of the girls, Moosa ﷺ could not bear.

So he stepped forward and asked them how they did fare.

They were unable to water their flock, Moosa ﷺ was told,

Not until the others had finished, as their father was old.[103]

So he watered their animals for them; then took shade under a tree.

He prayed, *"My Lord! I am in need of whatever good you send down on me."*

Meanwhile the two girls had returned home with their flock.

When they returned earlier than usual their father got a shock.

He learnt, their animals, a man had helped them to feed.

He sent his daughter to call him; wanting to repay him for helping those in need.

When she reached Moosa 🕊, he was tired and hungry; under a tree he lay.

She told him her father wanted to repay him for his help that day.

Moosa Finds a Home

Moosa 🕊 went to her aged father; of his story they did talk.[104]

The father said, *"Fear not, you have been saved from the oppressive folk."*

One of his daughters told him that Moosa 🕊 they should hire,

For the best labourer is one who is strong and not a liar.[105]

The father proposed, *"For eight years' service one of my daughters will marry you,*

You can complete ten years if you want, that will be the dowry which is due."

To this proposal of his, homeless Moosa 🕊 decided to agree,

He said, *"Whichever one I fulfil, there will be no injustice to me."*

In the Valley of Tuwa

Working in Madyan, those years Moosa 🕊 spent,

After which away with his family he went.

One cold dark night, a bright burning fire he saw.

Telling his family to wait, to the fire he did go.

He wanted to bring back some fire or find the right way,

Upon reaching the bright light, he heard a voice say:

"O Moosa! Indeed I am the Lord of the worlds," it called,

"Remove your shoes, you are in the holy valley of Tuwa," he was told.

The Miracles of Moosa ﷺ

He was ordered to listen carefully to that which is said,

As Allah intended that by him on the right path man be led.

"What is in your right hand, O Moosa?" Allah did ask.

Moosa ﷺ said, "It's my staff;" then explained how it helps him in his daily task.

Allah commanded Moosa ﷺ to throw his staff to the ground.

Suddenly in its place, a live running snake Moosa ﷺ found.

Naturally, he turned to run away when the snake he saw.

Allah said, "Take it and fear not, we will make it as it was before."[106]

Allah gave Moosa ﷺ another sign, so that Firown would see wrong from right.

When Moosa ﷺ put his hand under his arm, it would shine with a bright light.

To show Firown and his people these signs, Allah did command.

Teach them the true faith; the freedom Banu Isra'eel, he should demand.

Moosa ﷺ was afraid to go as one of their men he had killed.

So he prayed to Allah for help to accomplish what He willed.

Moosa ﷺ asked for a fluent tongue, as usually with a stutter he spoke.

And to have Haroon ﷺ, his brother, support him when to Firown he would talk.

Invitation to Firown

Moosa ﷺ and Haroon ﷺ went together to Firown's court,

From Firown, the freedom of Banu Isra'eel they sought.

They were now messengers of Allah, Firown was told,

They had been sent to tell him to leave his ways of old.

Moosa ﷺ showed him the miracle staff and his bright hand.

He replied, *"Have you come, O Moosa, to drive us out of our land?"*

Firown promised he would bring the same kind of magic too,

"So fix a time and a place that we shall not miss, nor will you."

The Contest

At a place where everyone could gather a date and time was set.

On a big open field, Moosa ﷺ, Firown and his magicians met.

The magicians asked Firown, *"If we win, what will our reward be?"*

Firown replied, *"You will surely be amongst those brought near to me."*

Moosa ﷺ warned the magicians that against Allah lies they should not invent.

Hearing his words, for a secret meeting the magicians went.

They said, *"These sorcerers have come to drive us out of our land.*

So arrange your rows, today we will be successful, the ones with the upper-hand."

They asked Moosa ﷺ, *"Will you throw first or shall we have our go."*

Moosa ﷺ told the sorcerers, *"Rather you throw."*

Over the eyes of the people, by the magicians, a spell was cast.

When they threw their sticks and ropes they seemed like snakes, moving fast.

Allah inspired Moosa ﷺ that his staff he must throw.

It turned into a snake which swallowed up the magic show.

The magicians were thus defeated and made low.

Of the truth about Moosa ﷺ, they now came to know.

They realised that Moosa ﷺ was true; so in prostration the magicians lay.

"We believe in the Lord of the universe, the Lord of Haroon and Moosa," they did say.

In broad daylight, the people saw Moosa ﷺ was truthful and Firown was a liar.

Firown announced, *"To lose the contest, to Moosa, the magicians did conspire."*[107]

Firown said, *"Do you believe in him before permission was granted by me?*

He is your chief who taught you magic; I shall cut your hands and feet alternately,

I shall crucify you on the trunks of a palm tree.

Then which of us is sterner and more lasting of punishment you will see."

The magicians had now become believers; Firown, no longer did they fear.

The worldly life and its luxuries, they no longer held dear.

They said, *"We will not give you preference to proofs which are clear.*

Do as you wish, for you will only end our life in this world here."

The Suffering of Banu Isra'eel

Only a small group believed in Moosa ﷺ; the others were scared.

To believe openly and oppose Firown not many dared.

The chiefs asked Firown, *"Will you let Moosa cause trouble in the land?"*

Some form of action against Banu Isra'eel, they did demand.

Again Firown resorted to his old plan, when all else fails.

He ordered the killing of all of Banu Isra'eel's baby males.

Banu Isra'eel were told to be patient; Allah's help they must seek.

But in their faith, Banu Isra'eel were still very weak.

They complained, *"We suffered hardship before you came,*

And after you have come, we endure the same."

Moosa ﷺ again told them to patiently wait,

"Your enemy, your Lord might soon annihilate."

Firown said, *"Leave me to kill Moosa, let him call to his Lord,*

I fear he will change your religion, and in the land cause discord."

A believing man of Firown's family, who kept his faith secret, said,

"For saying 'my Lord is Allah,' do you want this man dead?"

"And if he is a liar, his lies can do no harm to you.

Or that which he has threatened will strike you, if he is true.

O my people, you have the upper hand, the kingdom is yours today,

Who will save us from the wrath of Allah, if it came?" the believer did say.

Firown interrupted him and cut the believer's speech short.

"I only show you what I think, and guide you to right," Firown did retort.

The believer replied, *"I fear for you a fate like the groups of old,*

And, O my people, I fear the day when for reckoning you will be called."

Firown argued his case by claiming to be the Lord most-high.

And he commanded his people that Moosa ﷺ they must defy.

He stated, *"Is the kingdom of Egypt not mine, and the rivers that flow beneath me,*

And am I not better than this despicable man who cannot speak clearly?"

The Plagues

If he did not change his ways, of a punishment, Firown was warned.

But Firown refused; Moosa ﷺ and his mission he scorned.

Allah punished them with famine first and after that the flood.

They still disbelieved, so they were plagued with locusts, vermin, frogs and blood.

One after the other when these punishments came,

Upon Moosa ﷺ and those with him, they would put the blame.

When they could no longer bear it, to Moosa ﷺ, they would go.

So Allah would remove it, but they would remain the same as before.[108]

Banu Isra'eel Flee

When Firown and his people refused to believe,

Allah commanded Moosa ﷺ and Banu Isra'eel to leave.

Moosa ﷺ left with his people, under the cover of the night,

Where they could remain hidden and out of sight.

Banu Isra'eel travelled quickly; they wanted to be free.

They carried on travelling until they reached the Red Sea.

To get across the water, Banu Isra'eel could not find a way.

The darkness of the night was fading into the day.

Firown came to know of Banu Isra'eel's flight.

He gathered his army and set out to fight.

Firown was infuriated that they had decided to flee.

At dawn, he caught up with them by the Red Sea.

Banu Isra'eel were cornered; they had nowhere to go.

They knew that mercy, to them, Firown will not show.

Moosa صلى الله عليه وسلم consoled them that Allah's promise is true,

From Firown and his army, He will surely save you.

As Firown approached them the situation seemed dire.

Moosa صلى الله عليه وسلم struck the sea with his staff, as Allah did inspire.

The waters separated leaving a path, dry and clear.

Firown and his large army were now very near.

Banu Isra'eel rushed along this path with their children and family,

Whilst Firown and his army followed them into the sea.

The waters closed when Banu Isra'eel reached the other shore,

Firown and his army drowned; they were no more.

When Firown was drowning, the angels of punishment did appear.

Now the truth of Moosa's ﷺ words, to him, became very clear.

He screamed, *"In the one Allah of Banu Isra'eel, I believe."*

But it was too late now, from this world it was his time to leave.

The sea spat out Firown's body by Allah's command,

Nor was his dead corpse accepted by the land.

Allah preserved his body so that it may be a sign.

This is what happened to the man who claimed to be divine.

In the Desert

Banu Isra'eel saw the bodies of the army, washed ashore; dead.

After which into the wilderness, towards Sinai, they were led.

There, people worshipping statues and images they saw.

To have a god made for them, to worship, they asked for.

Moosa ﷺ was infuriated at their ingratitude; Banu Isra'eel he did scold.

"How can you seek a god other than Allah?" they were told.

Into the scorching hot desert without food or water they went.

But from the heavens, for them, many miracles were sent.

Clouds would follow them to shade them from the desert's heat.

Every day they would get heaven's mann and salwa to eat.[109]

Twelve springs would gush forth, when Moosa ﷺ struck a rock.

There was one spring each for every tribe of Banu Isra'eel and its flock.

Moosa ﷺ would strike a rock with his staff, when water they did need,

They delved deeper into the desert, with Moosa ﷺ as their lead.

Ungratefully they started complaining about eating the same food each day,

"We want herbs, cucumbers, corn, lentils and onions," they did say.

Moosa ﷺ was greatly annoyed and was now in a bad mood,

He said, *"Do you change that which is excellent for inferior food?*

If you want this then you will have to go live in settled land.

There you will get that which you demand."

Moosa ﷺ Talks with Allah

The time had now come to live by divine law.

Allah told Moosa ﷺ to Mount Sinai he should go.

"Take my place amongst the people," to Haroon ﷺ he did say,

"Do right and do not follow the mischief-makers way."

After fasting for thirty days, to his Lord he went to communicate.

To get rid of the smell of his mouth, some fragrant herbs he ate.

But to Allah the smell of a fasting person's mouth is not bad,

So Moosa ﷺ was told that another ten days of seclusion he should add.

Blessed by being able to talk to Allah, Allah he wanted to see.

But he received the answer, *"You do not have the strength to see Me.*

If you insist then over that mountain, We will reveal a glimpse of Our light.

If you can bear this, then again I will grant you my sight."

The mountain crumbled when Allah revealed a glimpse of his light,

Moosa ﷺ passed out; to see Allah he did not possess the might.

He said, *"Glory be to You, I turn to You repentant,"* when he awoke.

Moosa ﷺ became well-known as 'the one with whom Allah did talk.'

The Golden Calf

Moosa ﷺ received the Torah; whilst he was away

A man named Samiri had led Banu Isra'eel astray.

He collected the ornaments from the Jews and melted the gold.

He shaped it into a calf; *"This is your Lord,"* they were told.

He had put into it a handful of dust, which he had picked up from the ground.

This gave it a semblance of life and it would make a bleating sound.

Haroon ﷺ exclaimed, *"You are being tested with this, do you not see?*

Verily your Lord is ar-Rahman, so follow me."

But they carried on worshipping the calf; Haroon ﷺ they refused to obey.

"We will carry on worshipping this until Moosa returns," they did say.

Allah informed Moosa ﷺ, by Samiri, his people had been misled.

So Moosa ﷺ returned; *"Has your Lord not promised you a fair promise?"* he said.

"What do you have to say?" he then asked Samiri.

He replied, *"I perceived that which they did not see."*

When Banu Isra'eel were crossing the Red Sea,

Jibra'eel ﷺ came between them and the enemy.

Samiri had picked up some dust from under Jibra'eel's ﷺ feet.

And he cast this dust into the calf, which made it bleat.

Moosa ﷺ said, *"Go, and for you is to say, 'Do not touch me.'*

We will burn your god and scatter its ashes into the sea."

Moosa ﷺ asked Allah, 'what should be done to those who committed this sin?'

Allah commanded that all of them should be killed by the nearest of kin.

After this, for forgiveness from Allah, they were told to pray.

"He will accept your repentance; verily He is relenting, merciful," Moosa ﷺ did say

The Stubborn Nation

Banu Isra'eel accused Moosa ﷺ that from Allah the Torah he did not receive.

Moosa ﷺ chose seventy men to go to the mountain, so they believe.

But they quipped, *"When we see Allah, only then faith we will bring."*

Due to their stubbornness they were struck with an earthquake and lightning.

The foolish seventy men lay on the ground; dead.

"O Allah, forgive us, have mercy on us," Moosa ﷺ said.

Allah replied, *"My mercy encompasses everything."*

The seventy men from death back to life, He did bring.

When they returned they confirmed that Moosa ﷺ was true.

But again Banu Isra'eel answered, *"We don't believe you."*

Above their heads, Allah uprooted and lifted Mount Sinai.

This amazing portent proved that Moosa ﷺ did not lie.

Above Banu Isra'eel's heads, Mount Sinai towered

Fearing it would fall on them, Banu Isra'eel cowered.

To believe and act upon the Torah, they were told.

But after some time, they resorted to their ways of old.

The Exile

Banu Isra'eel had now reached their promised destination; the Holy Land.

"*Go and fight the inhabitants, do not turn and flee,*" Moosa ﷺ did command.

Though they were promised help from Allah, they feared the enemies might.

The people said, "*O Moosa, we will not go, you and your Lord go fight.*"

Moosa ﷺ asked Allah if from these people he could separate.

But Allah, the Just, had decided for them a different fate.

From entering the Holy Land, for forty years they were banned.

For that period of time they had to wander in the land.

He who considers deception as an art has in reality deceived himself.

Qaroon the Rich

Qaroon was a very wealthy man; he was Moosa's ﷺ relative.

A high status he had and a luxurious life he did live.

A group of mighty youths were needed to carry the keys to his treasure.

The wealth Qaroon had gathered was beyond measure.

He was told, *"Do good to others, as Allah has done good to you,*

Seek the abode of the hereafter, give everyone what they are due."

But Qaroon refused to give charity and to help those in need.

For the riches of this world, his heart was filled with greed.

Qaroon would reply, *"I have been given this for the knowledge I possess."*

He wouldn't give in charity, fearing his wealth would get less.

To show off his wealth, he went out in front of everyone one day,

"If only we had what has been given to Qaroon," some people did say.

The wise amongst the people told them not to desire such a thing,

Believing in Allah and doing good deeds; a better reward these bring.

Allah caused the earth to swallow Qaroon, his wealth and his dwelling.

For not being given what Qaroon had, Allah's praises the people did sing.

To leave this world we have come, for we were born to die one day.

The Quest for Knowledge

After Moosa ﷺ had given a sermon to Banu Isra'eel one day.

"Who is the most knowledgeable person?" someone did say.

To this Moosa ﷺ replied, *"Most knowledgeable am I."*

Allah reprimanded him for it; though it wasn't a lie.[110]

Compared to others, Allah had given Moosa ﷺ more.

So he should have attributed to Allah what he did know.

Allah told him of a knowledgeable servant where two seas meet.[111]

This more knowledgeable man, Moosa ﷺ wanted to greet.[112]

To go to learn from him, Moosa ﷺ made known his wish.

He was told by Allah that in a pot he should take a fish.

Where he loses the fish that is where the man would be.

So he travelled with Yusha bin Noon ﷺ to that point in the sea.

On the journey they stopped at a boulder; here Moosa ﷺ slept.

Suddenly the fish started moving and into the sea it leapt.

Yusha ﷺ was surprised at how the fish had left the pot.

But to mention this strange incident, Yusha ﷺ forgot.

They carried on journeying away from the place which they sought.

In the morning Moosa ﷺ, asked for his breakfast to be brought.

They had not felt tired on this journey of theirs before,

Until they had passed the place they had been told to go.

Yusha ﷺ then recollected what had happened when they had rested by the rock.

Shaytaan had made him forget the way the fish had given him a shock.

Moosa ﷺ calmly said, *"That was the place we were looking for."*

Tracing back their steps, they returned to the boulder once more.

There they found Khidr ﷺ, who was wrapped in a cloak.

With regards to the reason of Moosa's ﷺ travel they spoke.

Moosa ﷺ told him he was Moosa ﷺ of Banu Isra'eel; he asked what he sought,

That he wanted to accompany Khidr ﷺ, to learn what he had been taught.

Khidr ﷺ, who knew some of the future, said, *"Patient you will not be able to be."*

But Moosa ﷺ was adamant and replied, *"If Allah wills, patient you will find me."*

Khidr ﷺ knew he would not be patient; what he knew, Moosa ﷺ did not know.

He allowed him saying he shouldn't question him until the reason he did show.

Whilst walking along the shore, a ship happened to pass their way.

Upon recognising Khidr ﷺ, they let them board without having to pay.

Whilst journeying on the ship, a plank of wood, Khidr ﷺ decided to rip.

Moosa ﷺ scolded him saying, *"Do you want to drown the people of the ship?"*

He was perturbed at what Khidr ﷺ did; they hadn't made them pay.

Khidr ﷺ replied, *"You would not be able to be patient, did I not say?"*

Saying he had forgotten, Moosa ﷺ excused himself quickly.

And requested Khidr ﷺ, with him, harsh he should not be.

They had left the ship and they were on their way,

When they passed a child with whom two others did play.

Suddenly Khidr ﷺ grabbed the young child by his head,

And ripped it off with his hands; the child was dead.

Moosa was shocked that Khidr ﷺ killed a child, innocent and small.

And he thought Khidr ﷺ had killed him for no reason at all.

Khidr ﷺ reprimanded him, for not being patient, more severely than before.

Moosa ﷺ said, *"If I ask anything again, then do not accompany me anymore."*

Whilst travelling, to a village the two of them did go.

When they asked for food, the villagers said, "No".

In the village, they saw a wall which was about to fall.

Khidr ﷺ passed his hand over it and miraculously repaired the wall.

Moosa ﷺ said, *"They refused to host us or give us food to eat."*

He told him they could have got paid for this miraculous feat.

Khidr ﷺ said, *"This is where we separate and you go your own way."*

"I will tell you about that which you could not bear patience," he did say.

He explained that the ship belonged to some poor men who worked at sea.

Behind them was a king who took faultless ships oppressively.

The king left the ship alone when the hole he saw.

The poor men fixed it up after the king let them go.

As for the child he would have led his parents astray; thus he was killed.

To give them a better child in exchange is what Allah had willed.[113]

Pious parents of two orphans had hidden wealth for them under the wall.

Allah wanted to keep it hidden and safe, as the children were still small.[114]

Allah's Knowledge

Whilst they were travelling , a sparrow sat on the edge of the ship.

To drink some water, in the sea, its beak the sparrow did dip.

Khidr ﷺ said, *"Nothing decreased from Allah's knowledge by what he gave to you and me,*

Except for the example of how much water the sparrow just decreased from the sea." [115]

Intelligence is overrated, wisdom is not.

The Murder in Banu Isra'eel

Once, in Banu Isra'eel, a murder took place.

The culprit, nobody was able to trace.

On each other, people started to put the blame.

To resolve the matter, to Moosa ﷺ, they came.

To sort it out before it turned into a row,

Allah told Moosa ﷺ, they should slaughter a cow.

Banu Isra'eel replied, *"Do you take us as a joke?"*

Moosa ﷺ said, *"Allah forbid, that I should be from the ignorant folk."*

As usual Banu Isra'eel started to ask questions like 'how?'

Being unable to understand what it had to do with slaughtering a cow.

Any kind of cow would have been sufficient up to here,

But they told Moosa ﷺ to ask Allah to make the description more clear.[116]

Moosa ﷺ said, *"It should not be immature nor should it be due.*

Allah says that it should be in between the two."

Any kind of this cow would have been sufficient up to here,

But they told Moosa ﷺ to ask Allah to make the colour more clear.

They were told, in its colour, it should be yellow,

To the lookers sight, it should be mellow.

"Ask what kind, for cows look the same," they said,

"Lo, if Allah wills, aright we will be led."

They would have kept asking questions had they not said 'if Allah willed'.

They were told, *"It should be such a cow, by it, the earth had not been tilled.*

It can't have watered the fields, nor have a mark of any kind."

Now a cow of this specific description was very hard to find.

After a long search, they finally found the cow they sought,

It was a rare and unique cow; for a large sum it had to be bought.

Allah gave life to the murdered man when he was struck with a part of the cow.

He named the man who had killed him; they knew the murderer now.

The Runaway Stone

When Banu Isra'eel would bathe, clothes they wouldn't wear,

Out of modesty Moosa ﷺ would bathe when nobody was there.

Banu Isra'eel assumed, some defect of his body, he wanted to hide.

In reality, from seeing others unclothed, Moosa ﷺ shied.

One day when he was bathing alone,

He had put his clothes on a stone.

Taking his clothes, the stone ran away.

"My clothes, O stone!" Moosa ﷺ did say.

With Moosa ﷺ running behind it, the stone did flee,

Until unclothed Moosa ﷺ, a group of Banu Isra'eel did see.

In order to free Moosa ﷺ from their trouble, Allah did wish.

They exclaimed, *"By Allah, on Moosa there is no blemish."*

When the people said this, the stone came to a halt.

As they realised that Moosa ﷺ had no illness or fault.

From Banu Isra'eel he tolerated a lot of pain.

He persevered with patience again and again.

The value of all humans is equal in death. Why then is the value of all human life not considered equal?

An Encounter with Death

The Angel of Death came to Moosa ﷺ, when it was his time to die.

Moosa ﷺ slapped him so hard that he popped the angel's eye.[117]

Complaining about what Moosa ﷺ had done, back to Allah he did fly.

He protested, *"You sent me to a servant who does not want to die."*

After healing the angel's eye, to go back, Allah did command.

Allah told him to tell Moosa ﷺ, *"On the back of a bull put your hand."*

And for every hair which the hand covers, Allah would give

His noble messenger, Moosa ﷺ, an extra year to live.[118]

"O my Lord, then what?" Moosa ﷺ did reply.

Allah told him, *"After that you will die."*

Rather than get a year for each hair that comes under his hand,

He asked for death when he would be a stone throw away from the Holy Land.

One man's kindness to another man is what makes us mankind.

Yusha عَلَيْهِ السَّلَام

The youth who went with Moosa ﷺ to Khidr ﷺ was Yusha ﷺ.

He was the messenger of Banu Isra'eel, after Moosa ﷺ.

Wandering, Banu Isra'eel now needed a place to settle.

Previously, to fight for a home, they did not have the mettle.

Now, with Yusha ﷺ, their enemy they did defeat.

They were told to go into the town and freely eat.

Saying, "Repentance" they were told to enter the gate.

With humility and repentance they should prostrate.

Banu Isra'eel went in haughtily and with pride instead.

Changing the words they were supposed to have said.[119]

They entered defiantly, dragging their behinds on the path.

From the heavens, Allah sent down upon them His wrath.

It is the height of foolishness of the foolish one to question the wisdom of the wise.

Hizkiel علیہ السلام

It is said that during his apostleship, this incident took place.

The people of Banu Isra'eel had a difficult enemy to face.

Fearing death, in their thousands, from their homes they fled.

Allah said to them *'die'*; they all fell down dead.

They were then brought back to life, as Allah decreed,

So that others can learn a lesson, and take heed.

Nobody can avoid that which Allah did decree.

Nor should anyone fear the enemy, and flee.

The value of all humans is equal in death. Why then is the value of all human life not considered equal?

Ilyas

The people of Ilyas ﷺ had gone astray.

Ilyas ﷺ was sent to show them the right way.

He said, to his people, *"Do you not fear?"*

But in their hearts the idol Ba'al was dear.

Ilyas ﷺ asked, *"Leaving the best Creator, Ba'al do you call?"*

"Allah is your Lord and the Lord of us all."

By the people, Ilyas ﷺ and his message were rejected.

They will be presented to Allah when they are resurrected.

Unity ties U N I together.

Al-Yasa

Back to Yusuf ﷺ, his noble lineage goes.

To make him a messenger, Almighty Allah chose.

He was given apostleship, after Ilyas ﷺ was dead.

In the same manner as Ilyas ﷺ, Banu Isra'eel he led.

How stars beautify the dark sky so too does good character beautify man who is enshrouded in the
darkness of his sins.

Shamuil عَلَيْهِ السَّلَام

The Appointed King

By their enemies, Banu Isra'eel were being attacked.

The Tabernacle was stolen when the city was sacked.

Banu Isra'eel had had enough of being defeated.

They wanted victory and a change in how they were treated.

The leaders went to their messenger and asked for a king.

Shamuil عَلَيْهِ replied, *"What if you refrain from fighting?"*

They exclaimed, *"Why should we not fight in Allah's way?"*

"When with our children we've been driven out," they did say.

When they were told Allah had made Talut their king,

They complained that they were all more deserving.

They derided him, saying he was poor and did not possess wealth.

Shamuil عَلَيْهِ replied, *"Allah has given him wisdom and good health."*

"The sign that Allah has appointed him as king,

Is the Tabernacle back to you the angels will bring.

In it tranquillity from your Lord you will find,

And remnants of what Moosa and Haroon left behind."

Banu Isra'eel Go to War

Angels carrying the Tabernacle back, they saw.

Now they realised Talut would win them the war.

Talut set out with the army; they were put to a test.

From the men in the army, it would pick out the best.

Not to drink the water from the river, Allah did command,

They were allowed to drink a scoop of water with one hand.

But they all drank to their fill from the river, except for a few.

Those who drank were separated, for in courage they were untrue.

The army was now like that of the Muslims of Badr in number.[120]

They crossed the river; upon seeing Jalut, they did encumber.

When they saw the size of the army, Banu Isra'eel began to cower.

They said, *"To fight Jalut and his army, we do not possess the power."*

Though death is inevitable, youth seems eternal.

Dawood عليه السلام

The Young Hero

A challenge by Jalut, to the Isra'eeli forces, was thrown.

For his strength and brute force, he was well known.

To come forward and face him nobody dared.

To meet the challenge, Banu Isra'eel were scared.

Suddenly a young boy appeared on the scene.

He seemed no match for Jalut; he was healthy but lean.

The boy attacked the giant Jalut so fast,

He could not defend himself; Jalut breathed his last.

This amazing feat of bravery became of great fame.

He was from a common family, Dawood عليه السلام was his name.

Talut had promised the winner, in marriage, his daughter's hand.

And after him the winner would be appointed king of the land.

Dawood عليه السلام, the Vicegerent

To Dawood عليه السلام, the Zaboor Allah did reveal,

Which he read melodiously with great zeal.

Upon hearing his voice, around him birds soared.

The mountains and birds joined him in praising the Lord.

He used to keep a fast every other day,

And for one third of the night he would pray.

Allah made iron soft and flexible in his hand

With great piety and justice he ruled the land.

Oft repenting; to his Lord he would turn.

Though he was a king he would work to earn.

To his wife, a son, Sulayman ﷺ was born.

He became a messenger and successor to his throne

Dawood's ﷺ Test in Judgement

Once Dawood ﷺ was praying in his room; it had been locked.

Two men climbed the wall into his room; Dawood ﷺ was shocked.

Seeing him terrified, they said, *"Do not fear.*

For a judgement in our case we are here"

'One of us has done injustice to the other.'

One of them spoke, *"This is my brother.*

I have one ewe and ninety-nine ewes has he.

Being better in speech, he said hand it over to me."

Dawood ﷺ said, without listening to his brother,

"You have done wrong to ask him for his ewe.

Many partners oppress one another,

Except for the righteous, and they are few."

He had not listened to the other side,

By Allah he was being tested and tried.[121]

But the men had gone; he realised too late.

Repenting to his Lord, he fell down prostrate.

An Incident

Adam's 🕮 offspring were taken from his backbone.[122]

All of his future children, to him were shown.

He saw a handsome man, who had a shining forehead.

"Who is this youth?" curious Adam 🕮 said.

He was told it is Dawood 🕮, and for sixty years he would live.

Adam 🕮 said forty years from his life to this youth he wanted to give.

When Death's Angel came to take his life, *"I still have forty years,"* he did say.

Death's Angel reminded him that, to Dawood 🕮, he had given these years away.

How stars beautify the dark sky so too does good character beautify man who is enshrouded in the
darkness of his sins.

Sulayman عليه السلام

Sulayman عليه السلام was a powerful and great king.

Allah had gifted him with a miraculous ring.

He was a wise messenger and very just.

Allah granted him a large kingdom as a trust.

Whose Baby is it?

Two women wanted justice; to Dawood عليه السلام they came.

To being the mother of one child, both of them did claim.

To the elder of the two, his father gave the son.

But Sulayman عليه السلام felt justice had not been done.

By Sulayman عليه السلام, the executioner was called.

"Cut the child in two," the executioner he told.

"It belongs to her!" screamed the younger of the two.

Seeing her reaction, it was the young woman's he knew.[123]

The Sheep and the Crops

For judgement in their matter, to Dawood عليه السلام, two men came.

For eating his crops, the other man's sheep, one did blame.

For the eaten crops, his father gave the other's sheep in lieu.

But Sulayman عليه السلام thought that a different justice was due.

To the man who lost his crops, he gave the sheep.

Until his crops grew back, the sheep he could keep.

With the sheep, he could do as he willed.

Until, to their original form, his crops were tilled.[124]

Sulayman's ﷺ Wish

One day, Sulayman ﷺ said, *"I will go to each of my seventy wives tonight,*

So that they may give birth to knights, who in Allah's path will fight."

One of his companions reminded him to say 'if has Allah willed'.

But Sulayman's ﷺ desire was not going to be fulfilled.[125]

To say the words of his companion, he forgot.

So except for one, the rest of his wives conceived not.

She gave birth to a child with part of its body missing.

Allah was testing Sulayman ﷺ, the just king.

By Allah, the Messenger Sulayman ﷺ was tested.[126]

On his great embellished throne, a mere body rested.

"My Lord, forgive me and grant me a kingdom," said he,

"Such as will not belong to anyone after me."

Sulayman's ﷺ Kingdom

An army of men, jinn, birds and animals he did command,

With which, for Allah's pleasure, he conquered the land.

In any direction and with any force, he could make the wind blow.

When he required metal, out of the ground copper would flow.[127]

Once he was marching with his forces, armed,

When a colony of ants fled so they remain unharmed.

He smiled when he heard an ant tell her colony to flee.

She warned them, they might be crushed if the army does not see.

The Queen of Sheba

One day, without his permission, a hoopoe had gone.[128]

He said, *"It will be disciplined, if it has reason none."*

Upon returning, the hoopoe reported what it had seen,

'Worshippers of the sun, the people and their queen.'

To worship one Lord, to the queen a letter he wrote,

Which told them to come to us as believers, to avoid a war being fought.

When he completed the letter he gave it to the hoopoe.

To deliver the letter to the queen, the hoopoe did go.

The hoopoe returned to the place where he had been.

He delivered the letter to the surprised queen.

The queen was perplexed when she read the letters content.

Not sure what action to take for her ministers she sent.

For advice from her ministers, the Queen of Sheba asked for.

They told her that, if she commanded them, they were ready for war.

But to avoid a war, to Sulayman ﷺ, gifts were sent.[129]

With gifts for Sulayman ﷺ, the queen's envoys went.

When they gave him the gifts, *"Do you provide me with wealth,"* said he.

"Compared to what has been given to you, Allah has given better to me.

Rather you enjoy your gifts;" the queen's gifts, Sulayman ﷺ did spurn.

With an army, they would be powerless against, he promised to return.

"Who will bring her throne to me?" his subjects he did ask,

Ifrit, a mischievous jinn, was willing to take up the task,

Without the queen realising, he had to bring the throne,

When she arrived would she recognise it as her own?

Ifrit offered to bring the throne, before Sulayman ﷺ does rise,

Said another, *"I will bring it in the twinkling of one's eyes."*

He brought the throne forth by mentioning Allah's great name.[130]

To Sulayman's ﷺ palace, the Queen of Sheba now came.

The truth of the matter Sulayman ﷺ wanted to teach.

So he tested the queen, when the palace she did reach.

"Is your throne like this?" she was asked when she came.

She replied, *"It is as though it is the very same."*

In Sulayman's ﷺ palace, there was a beautiful glass floor.

The glass could not be seen; under it water did flow.

Thinking the glass floor was a pool, she lifted her gown.

She was told it was covered with glass, so she put it back down.

She recognised Allah's power through the glass floor and her throne,

She and her people took up the worship of one Allah alone.

Before, she believed that things grew because of the sun,

Now she believed that it was Allah who makes everything happen. [131]

The Death of Sulayman ﷺ

By the jinn, Sulayman ﷺ was not allowed to be seen.

He would supervise them, whilst on his staff he would lean.

If they glanced back or if at him they were to gaze,

Then, in the alcove, that jinn would die in a fiery blaze.

Once, a jinn glanced back and he was not burnt.

Only then of the death of Sulayman ﷺ they learnt.

An insect had gnawed at his staff's wood.

Finally his staff fell; Sulayman ﷺ no longer stood.

About knowing the unseen, the Jinn had lied.

They did not know that Sulayman ﷺ had died.

The death of Sulayman ﷺ, the Jinn never saw.

He had passed away a long time before. [132]

Ilm (knowledge) is an everlasting candle which does not benefit unless lit with the flame of aml (acting upon it).

Uzair عَلَيْهِ السَّلاَم

Once Uzair ﷺ was travelling, he passed by a ruined town.

At this place, to eat his food, from his donkey he got down.

"How will Allah bring this to life after its death?" he said.

Allah caused him to die; for a hundred years in this place he lay dead.

When Allah revived him, *"How long have you remained?"* He did say.

Uzair ﷺ replied, *"I have remained a day or part of a day."*

Uzair ﷺ felt that for very long he had not laid.

Allah said, *"Rather, for one hundred years, you have stayed."*

"Look at your food and drink," he was told.

With the passage of time, it had not gone old.

But his donkey had died and was dust and bone.

The power of giving life to the dead was to be shown.

The donkey had died, whilst the food had stayed fresh.

Allah raised the donkey's bones and covered them with flesh.

Uzair ﷺ saw how Allah was capable of all things divine.[133]

For the people, Allah made Uzair's ﷺ life a sign.[134]

The Birth of Maryam ﷺ

The Birth of Maryam ﷺ

In Banu Isra'eel, there lived a pious man.

He was well-respected; his name was Imran.

A child, both Imran and his wife did desire.

In asking from Allah, his wife never did tire.

For a good and obedient child, she would regularly supplicate.

Her son, to the service of Masjid ul-Aqsa, she vowed to dedicate.

Unfortunately, before the child was born, Imran passed away.

Hannah ﷺ gave birth to the child, for which she used to pray. [135]

Hannah's emotions turned, to confusion, from joy.

Her baby was a girl; she had been expecting a boy.

With a girl how was her vow going to be fulfilled?

She took comfort in the fact that this is what Allah willed.

The Carer of Maryam ﷺ

She would fulfil her vow; to the Masjid, Maryam ﷺ would be sent.

When Maryam ﷺ was older, to the clergy of al-Aqsa she went.[136]

Who would care for Maryam ﷺ, since her father had died?

For the honour of caring for Maryam ﷺ, all the clergy vied.

Of the clergy, the Messenger Zakariyya ﷺ was the head.

"The honour of looking after her belongs to me," he said.

To the aunt of Maryam ﷺ, Zakariyya ﷺ was married.

But they kept debating; in deciding they tarried.

To bring an end to the problem, to the river Allah told them to go.

Here the person, who would look after Maryam ﷺ, Allah would show.

Their pens into the river, the competing clergy were told to throw.

The carer would be the one whose pen in the opposite direction did flow.

Against the flow of the current, went Zakariyya's ﷺ pen,

Whilst floated down the river, the pens of the other men.

He was entrusted with Maryam ﷺ, who was placed under his care.

He gave her a room, in which he would go to see how she did fare.

The Miraculous Fruit

Into a pious and Allah-fearing lady, Maryam ﷞ grew.

In her room, the worship of Allah she would do.

Zakariyya ﷡ found by her out of season fruits, one day.

"O Maryam, where have you got this from?" he did say.

"This is from Allah," the pious lady, Maryam ﷞, replied.

Zakariyya ﷡ thought 'if out of season fruits Allah does provide,

Then Allah has the power to give me a child, though I am old.'

"Give me a pious child," unto his Almighty Lord he called.[137]

Fulfilling your needs will satiate you, whilst fulfilling your desires will make you hungrier.

Zakariyya علیه السلام

Zakariyya's علیه السلام Prayer

A story of Zakariyya علیه السلام in the Qur'an we are told.

He was a messenger of Banu Isra'eel, and was very old.

His wife was barren; old age she had reached.

For a child, to carry on after him, to Allah he beseeched.

In secret, to his Lord, Zakariyya علیه السلام did pray,

"My bones are feeble and my head glistens with grey,

Never has my prayer to you gone unanswered before."

Great humbleness and servitude to Allah, he did show.

He feared for his relatives; he worried how they would fare.

So he asked Allah the Almighty for an heir.

A son who would inherit his knowledge and prophethood,

One with whom Allah is pleased, as he is pious and good.

Glad Tidings of Yahya علیه السلام

Allah gave glad tidings to Zakariyya علیه السلام of the son for which he did implore.

His name would be Yahya علیه السلام; a name not given to anyone before.

"How can I have a son, my wife is barren and I have reached old age?" he said

He did not doubt the power of Allah; he doubted human ability instead.

Zakariyya ﷺ was told, *"So it will be.*

Your Lord says, 'It is easy for me'."

Zakariyya ﷺ to life, did Allah not bring,

When Zakariyya ﷺ had also been nothing?[138]

Zakariyya ﷺ, anticipating his son, requested, *"My Lord appoint for me a sign."*

Allah said, *"You will be unable to talk for three nights, though your body is fine."*

He came out of his mihrab, when the arrival of Yahya ﷺ was soon.

And he signed to the people to glorify Allah, in the morning and afternoon.[139]

Zakariyya's ﷺ Death

Banu Isra'eel decided to kill Zakariyya ﷺ; from them he did flee.

Zakariyya ﷺ hid himself inside the opening of a tree.

When the Isra'eelites realised that in the tree he did hide,

They sawed it in two; by Zakariyya ﷺ not a sigh of pain was cried. [140]

Don't destroy your shack because of your neighbour's castle.

Yahya

Yahya ﷺ, the Kind

Yahya ﷺ was a miracle; to old parents he was born.

To them, by him, obedience and great love was shown.

Allah ordered him, 'To the scriptures you must hold fast.'

In wisdom and piety, the children of the time he surpassed.

Allah made him sympathetic to men as a mercy.

Pure from all sins and very righteous was he.

In the Qur'an for his kindness and obedience to his parents he is praised.

'Peace be upon him the day he was born, the day he dies and the day he is raised.'

To all living things, men and animals, Yahya ﷺ was kind.

In the solitude of the wilderness, peace he did find.

Out of fear of Allah, he would constantly weep.

Due to his love for Allah, he found it difficult to sleep.

Yahya's ﷺ Death

There ruled a tyrant king; Herod was his name.

With his beautiful niece, infatuated he became.

People would not speak out because they were in awe.

But Yahya ﷺ said the relationship went against the Tawrat's law.

One day he told his niece, 'whatever she desires will be fulfilled.'

She wished for the Messenger Yahya ﷺ to be killed.

Herod fulfilled her request; Yahya ﷺ was unjustly executed.

Allah avenged Yahya ﷺ; by an army Herod's kingdom was looted.[141]

Fear that which is to come because of that which has gone.

Isa

Tidings of Isa ﷺ

Maryam ﷺ was engaged in worshipping Allah, night and day.

She was pure and pious; only to Allah she would pray.

Once, to the eastern part of the Masjid, for a bath she went.

To her, in human form, the Angel Jibra'eel ﷺ was sent.

Maryam ﷺ was deeply disturbed, when the stranger appeared.

Being a noble and chaste woman, the man she feared.

She cried, *"I seek Allah's protection, do not come near.*

Keep away from me, if Allah you fear."

Jibra'eel ﷺ said, *"I am a messenger from your Lord, to give you good news of a son."*

Maryam ﷺ replied, *"How can I have a son, when I have been touched by no-one?"*

He said, *"It is easy for Allah. He is to be a sign for mankind, so that they may take heed.*

And he is a mercy from Allah, it is a matter Allah has already decreed."

"Whilst still a baby, in the cradle, he will be able to speak.

He will answer the people, when questions about his birth they seek.

To become a great messenger of Banu Isra'eel he will live.

Allah will teach him the book; and great wisdom to him, He will give."

Maryam ﷺ had been chosen for a miracle that was great.

Allah showed, without a father, a child He can create.

Over what people would say, Maryam ﷺ did worry and grieve.

Bayt ul-Maqdis, she eventually decided to leave.

The Birth of Isa ﷺ

She travelled alone; exhausted to a mountain she came.

Today, Bayt ul-Laham (Bethlehem) is the town's name.

When she felt the pangs of birth, she took refuge under a date-tree.

And said, *"I wish I had died before this and everyone had forgotten me."*[142]

"Do not worry, your Lord has provided a water stream," she heard a voice call,

"And shake the trunk of the palm tree; fresh, ripe dates will fall."

Allah knew Maryam ﷺ was worried about what her people would say,

So she was told, *"Say, 'I have vowed a fast not to speak to anyone this day'."*

Isa's ﷺ First Words

When Maryam ﷺ returned, people saw that a baby she carried.

They were shocked and surprised, as Maryam ﷺ was unmarried.

They said, *"O Maryam, you have come with an amazing thing.*
Your parents were not bad; this child, from where did you bring?"

She did not answer; she pointed to the small child instead.
"How can we talk to a child, who is in the cradle?" they said.
To their amazement, *"I am the servant of Allah,"* Isa ﷺ replied.[143]
Baby Isa ﷺ proved, to the people, that his mother never lied.

"He has made me blessed wherever I may be.
And to perform salaah , he has commanded me.
And also zakah I should give
As long as I should live."

Amazed at hearing his words, they accepted him as a sign of Allah's might.

They dismissed their bad thoughts and believed Maryam ﷺ to be right.

As the years passed, into a righteous and noble man, Isa ﷺ did grow.

The world around had become corrupt and immoral, he saw.

Isa ﷺ Preaches the Truth

To the true teachings of the Tawrat, the religious leaders paid no heed.

They made what was wrong into right, and right into wrong, out of greed.

The scholars and priests desired that worldly possessions they should gain.

They changed the laws of the Tawrat; no longer did the original text remain.

Isa ﷽ said, "*I am human like the messengers before me, who were sent to guide too.*

Allah has revealed His book, the Injeel, to me and has sent me to reform you."

But Isa's ﷽ call towards good, the people refused to hear.

The religious leaders opposed him and people did mock and jeer.

The Miracles of Isa ﷽

The people demanded that Isa ﷽ perform miracles divine.

By his hands, Allah showed them many a sign.

He cured the sick, and brought back to life those who did die.

He would make a bird out of clay, blow life into it and it would fly.

He revealed to the people what they ate.

What was hidden in their homes, he would relate.

The eyesight of those born blind, he restored.

He did all these miracles with the permission of his Lord.

The Evil Plot

The leaders were worried that they would have to give up what they had amassed.

So they alleged Isa's ﷽ miracles were magic, and upon him doubts they cast.

Isa ﷽ travelled from place to place preaching, 'on the true religion hold fast'.

He also gave tidings of Ahmad ﷺ, of the messengers he would be the last.[144]

Though some rejected him, many accepted the true deen.

Those who helped him spread the religion were the Hawariyyeen.[145]

Towards Isa's ﷽ preaching, more and more people began to turn.

The leaders could not tolerate this; with jealousy they did burn.

They intended to kill him, a plot they soon did devise.

They went to the Roman Governor and fed him some lies.

They said, *"To be the King of the Isra'eelis, Isa does intend."*

The governor was convinced; to arrest Isa ﷺ, his soldiers he did send.

Allah informed Isa ﷺ of the plot and the order to have him arrested.

Isa ﷺ told his followers that very soon they were going to be tested.

He told them to carry on preaching after he was gone.

They promised to be helpers of the religion of Allah, the One.

Isa ﷺ Ascends

The house which Isa ﷺ was in, the soldiers did surround.

A man went inside, but Isa ﷺ could not be found.

Unable to find him, the man was fazed.

Up into the heavens, Isa ﷺ had been raised.

Whilst the man was searching for Isa's ﷺ trace,

To make him look like Isa ﷺ, Allah changed his face.

The soldiers went in when their man had not come out.

They arrested him, *"I am not Isa,"* the man did shout.[146]

Because he looked like Isa ﷺ, the soldiers thought he lied.

They thought, to save his life, the truth he denied.

The guards seized him, and on the cross he was crucified.

Isa ﷺ is alive in the heavens; he has not yet died.

The Second Coming of Isa (علیه السلام)

Close to Qiyamah, Dajjal will arrive.

To mislead Muslims, plots he will contrive.

He will only be able to see from one eye.

He will claim apostleship and then divinity; he will lie.[147]

The letters 'Ka Fa Ra' will be inscribed on his head.

True Muslims will testify he is a 'kafir', when these letters are read.

Dajjal will gather an army; the Muslims he will want to defeat.

Outside Damascus, in Syria, the two armies will meet.

Then suddenly, from the heavens, Isa (علیه السلام) will descend.

To the Muslims, a helping hand he will lend.

Isa (علیه السلام), on the battlefield, Dajjal will see.

Knowing he has been sent to kill him, Dajjal will flee.

Isa (علیه السلام) will chase him and Dajjal will be killed.

After which, with peace, the world will be filled.

During his rule, the Yajuj and Majuj will appear.[148]

This is a sign that Qiyamah is drawing near.

Havoc and destruction, the Yajuj and Majuj will cause.

The Muslims will seek refuge, on a mountain, from these foes.

Then the Yajuj and Majuj, Allah will destroy.

After which the world will be filled with happiness and joy.

Isa عليه السلام will not come as a new messenger, when he sent by Allah.

Rather he will come as an ummati; a follower of Rasulullah ﷺ.

People will start disbelieving in Allah, after Isa عليه السلام is dead.

Throughout the world disbelief, lies and sins will then spread.

Though one may turn a blind eye, it does not mean he is blind.

The Three Men from Banu Isra'eel

There were three men from Banu Isra'eel, one leper, one blind and one bald.

Allah wanted to test them, so to go to them an angel was told.

The angel went to the leper and asked, *"What is most beloved to you?"*

He replied, *"Good colour and skin, and that people stop telling me to shoo."*

The angel passed his hand over him and he was given good skin and health.

Then the angel asked, *"What is most beloved to you in terms of wealth?"*

"Camel," was his reply; the angel gave him a camel and prayed for it to be blessed.

Then the angel left the leper to see whether he would later pass the test.

Then he went to the bald man and asked, *"What is most beloved to you?"*

He replied, *"Beautiful hair and that people stop telling me to shoo."*

The angel passed his hand over him and he was given good hair and health.

Then the angel asked, *"What is most beloved to you in terms of wealth?"*

"Cow," was his reply; the angel gave him a cow and prayed for it to be blessed.

Then the angel left the leper to see whether he would later pass the test.

Then he went to the blind man and asked, *"What is most beloved to you?"*

He replied, *"That Allah gives me my sight back, so that I can see people too."*

The angel passed his hand over him and Allah returned his sight and health.

Then the angel asked, *"What is most beloved to you in terms of wealth?"*

He said, *"Goat;"* he was given a goat; all three's animals gave birth to many more.

When each of them had a valley full of animals, back to them the angel did go.

First to the leper, as a poor traveller, in an old state, the angel went.

He asked in Allah's name, who had given him all of this, if a camel could be lent.

He refused; the Angel asked, *"Aren't you the leper to whom Allah gave health and more?"*

He denied this; the angel said, *"If you're lying, may Allah make you as you were before."*

The same thing happened when to the bald man the angel did go.

So the angel said, *"If you are lying, may Allah make you as you were before."*

Then he went as a poor traveller to the one who used to be blind.

And asked for a goat as only Allah's and his help he could find.

Of being blind and poor, and that Allah had returned his sight, he admitted to.

He said, *"Take whatever you want, I will prevent nothing from you."*

The angel told him to keep his wealth; who was grateful, Allah wanted to see.

Allah was angry with his companions but with him Allah was happy.

Unity ties U N I together.

The Woman and the Dog

A bad woman from Banu Isra'eel once saw

A thirsty dog licking wet mud off the floor.

Though she did many a sin,

Allah's pleasure she did win,

From the well, for the dog, water she did draw.[149]

*If there is no **unity** in h**uma**n**ity** then all that remains are HMA; High Maintenance Animals.*

The Man Who Feared

Allah

A dying man from Banu Isra'eel told his sons to make a fire.

After he died they should burn him on the pyre.

Then on a windy day, in the sea, his ashes should be spread.

He was a sinner who feared being raised from the dead.

Allah gathered his ashes and then asked him, *"Why?"*

"Because of my fear for you", was the man's reply.[150]

Allah the most merciful forgave him for the fear he had.

Never become despondent of Allah's mercy, if you've been bad.

How stars beautify the dark sky so too does good character beautify man who is enshrouded in the darkness of his sins.

Definitions

Aa

abandon	to leave or give up
absurd	to find something foolish or unreasonable
abundant	a lot, many
abuse	to cause hurt, or not treat something or someone properly
accompany	to go with someone
accomplish	to complete, to finish something one set out to do
acknowledge	to recognize something, or to admit
acquiesce	to agree, or accept
adamant	not wanting to change your mind
address	to speak to
advance	to go forward
affair	a situation
affirmative	express agreement in the positive, yes
afflict	cause pain
afore	before
ahaadith	plural of hadith, a saying or act of the Messenger ﷺ.
aid	to help
alcove	an indention in the wall, sometimes for seclusion
alternately	every other, to happen after each other
amass	to gather in a large number
ambition	a goal which someone really wants to achieve
ambush	to attack someone by surprise
amidst	amongst
ancestor	the people from whom one is descended
annihilate	to destroy
anticipate	to wait for something
approach	to come close to
arid	land which does not have much vegetation and very little rain
aright	rightly or correctly
ark	a ship used as a sanctuary
arrogance	pride and thinking yourself better than others

ascertain	to find out the truth regarding a matter
ascribe	to attribute or credit someone with something
assist	to help with something
astray	to go off the right path
attempt	to try
attest	to bear witness
attire	clothing
attitude	the way a person behaves, feels or thinks
authority	someone in the position of power
avail	help
avenge	to take revenge
aware	to know and recognise something

Bb

bald	to have no hair
banquet	to feast
bar	to stop
bare	uncovered, not having anything or minimal amount
barren	unable to have a child, land which is unable to grow vegetation
bear	to tolerate
befit	to be appropriate
behove	to find appropriate
belief	to accept something as true, a firm conviction in the truth of a statement
bequest	a final request, or to leave something in for someone in ones will
beseech	to ask, to plead
besieger	one who lays siege
bestow	to grant, give
betray	to hand over something of trust to someone's enemy who considered you to be a friend
bleat	to make sheep like cry
blemish	fault
blessing	a favour
bore	to give birth

bound	to be tied, to go towards
brute	animal like, very strong
burden	a heavy load

Cc

capable	to be able to do something
caravan	olden times; the group of people who used to travel with camels and horses loaded with goods
cast	to throw
chaste	to be pure
cherish	to love
clan	a large extended family
comply	to do something according to how someone wishes
composition	made up of
comprehend	to understand
conceive	to come up with a plan, to be with child
confess	to admit
confide	to tell someone something in private and trust them not to tell anyone
consecutive	one after the other
consent	to give permission
console	to comfort someone who is sad
conspire	to make a plan to harm someone
content	what something consists of
contract	an agreement
contradict	to speak the opposite of what someone else said
contrive	to come up with
convey	to pass on something to someone, to get something across to someone
conviction	a firm belief,
convince	to cause someone to believe something
cope	to bear with
Copt	Egyptian
cornered	to have nowhere else to go
corruption	when people in power abuse their power and are dishonest
courtesy	to show politeness

cower	to be scared
crave	to strongly desire something, to want
crucify	to hang or nail someone on a cross
crude	rude, not have manners
culprit	one who has committed a crime
current	the direction in which the water flows, also means now

Dd

daily	everyday
dawn	the first light of day
deceive	to make someone believe something which is not true
decrease	to become less
decree	to order given by someone in power
dedicate	to commit oneself to something
deed	an action
deen	religion
defiant	to defy
delay	to make late
denounce	inform against something,
deplete	to use up, gradually finish
descend	to come down
descendant	to be the child of
desire	to want
desolate	to be empty
despair	to lose hope
despondent	to be sad having lost hope
destination	place where one wants to go
destined	what has already been planned by the creator
detain	to keep or hold back
devise	to come up with
devote	to be loyal, give oneself to something
devour	to eat up
diet	what one eats
deity	god
differentiate	to be able to tell the difference

diminish	to gradually decrease
dim	low level of light
dine	to eat
dire	a very serious situation
disbeliever	one who does not believe (is not a Muslim)
discern	to recognize
disclose	make something known
discord	disagreement between people
disfigure	to spoil something's appearance
disgrace	to lose respect, bring shame
dismiss	to order someone to leave
dismount	to get of an animal
despicable	bad
dispute	disagreement
distress	to be extremely worried or in pain
divine	from Allah
doubt	to be unsure
dowry	the money or goods given to a women on marriage
draw a lot	to take a random pick from a selection
draw water	to take water out of a well
dread	not looking forward to
drought	a shortage of water
due	something which needs to be given is said to be due
dutifully	to do something as one feels it is their duty to do so
dye	to colour

Ee

eager	to want to do something
eloquent	speech that is clear and persuasive
embellish	to make something more beautiful
emotion	a feeling
emphasize	to give greater importance to something
encompass	to include all areas, surround
encounter	to come across
encumber	to put a heavy load on someone or something

endure	to put up with
enquire	to ask
enslave	to make someone a slave of
ensure	to make sure
entice	to tempt someone by showing them the benefits
entrust	to give to someone in trust
envoy	a messenger who had been sent to deliver a message
equality	being equal, fair and just
era	a time-span
establish	to set up permanently
eternal	lasting forever
ewe	a female sheep
exchange	to give one thing for another
executioner	the one who kills people upon whom the death sentence has been passed
exert	to try hard
exile	being forbidden to return to a one's hometown
expedition	a journey taken by a group
expose	to show something up
express	to convey ones thoughts

Ff

faithful	loyal
famine	shortage of food
fast	known in Arabic as sawm. Not to eat, drink or engage in relations with one's spouse from dawn till sunset.
faze	to be of disturbance
feat	an achievement which requires an effort
feeble	weak
fend off	to fight off, or prevent
ferocious	fierce
fervour	to be emotionally excited
flaw	fault, mistake
flexible	to bend easily, to change easily
flock	a group of animals, the gathering of many people
fluent	to be able to speak clearly and easily get ones message

	across
foe	enemy
forefathers	an ancestor
forgiveness	to let go of an offence someone caused you
forsake	to leave
fortify	to make something strong
foundation	the base or ideal upon which everything else is built
frantically	hurriedly, anxiously and fearfully
frequent	often
feud	a quarrel which has lasted between two groups for a long period of time
furious	angry
futile	useless or pointless

Gg

glimpse	to sight a part of something, or to get a glance of something for a moment
glisten	shine
gratitude	to be thankful
guarantee	to assure or promise
guide	one who shows the way

Hh

halt	stop
hamstrung	cut the hamstrings
hardship	difficulty
harsh	severe
haste	hurry, to do an action very quickly
haughty	proud
Hawariyeen	Arabic for disciples
heart-rending	something which effects ones emotions
heed	to take notice of
heir	one who inherits after a person passes away
hesitate	to be wary of doing something
hire	to borrow or employ someone for money
honour	a lot of respect and esteem

Hoopoe	a species of bird
horde	a large group of people, to accumulate in great amounts
host	the one who looks after the guests needs
humanity	the human race
humble	to deem oneself as low
humility	humbleness, *see humble*

Ii

illuminate	light up
imaan	faith
immature	not yet an adult, childish
immoral	something which goes against what is generally accepted to be right
immortal	never dying
implore	to ask pleadingly
incident	something which has happened
incline	side towards something
increase	to become more
independent	not requiring the assistance of anyone
indicate	to point towards
indulge	to be engrossed in something
inevitable	something which is definitely going to occur
inferior	to be of less value
infuriate	to make angry
ingratitude	to be ungrateful
inhabitant	one who lives in a place is said to be its inhabitant
inherit	to acquire something on the death of someone
initially	at the beginning
Injeel	Arabic for the Gospel, the New Testament
innocent	to be free of fault, not guilty
inscribe	to write or engrave into something
insist	to demand, to not take no for an answer
insult	to cause offence
intend	what one plans to do
intense	severe

interpret	translate, to explain
invent	to come up with, to make up

Jj

Jibra'eel ﷺ	the Archangel, who used to bring messages of Allah to the messengers

Kk

kafir	a disbeliever
khadim	a helper, one who assists
kin	family and relatives
kith	friends

Ll

labourer	worker
lean	thin
leper	one who suffers from leprosy
lest	in case
liberate	to free
lieu	in exchange
lifeless	without life
lure	to make an attempt of getting something to go to a place you want
lust	desire

Mm

maintain	to keep up
malice	hatred, wanting to do something evil
mann	food from heaven given to Banu Isra'eel when they were wandering in the desert
manuscript	a book or document
martyr	one who has been killed in special cause, usually religious
measure	bowl with which one measures
meek	humble
mellow	pleasant
melodiously	with a pleasant tune
merchandise	goods
merciless	without mercy, unkind
merry	happy

migration	to leave one place for another
mihrab	the alcove in the wall, an area of seclusion
minor	small
miracle	a divine action which humans are not capable of doing
misconception	a view one has due to thinking or understanding something incorrectly
misfortune	bad luck
misguide	to be show the wrong way
mock	to make fun of something
modesty	to be moderate, humble
mourn	to grieve, be sad at the loss of something
mushrik	polytheist, one who believes in more than one god

Nn

nafs	Arabic for soul, the inner desire which directs a man
nation	a large group of people who have a common country, ancestor or history
norm	that which is normal

Oo

oath	a promise
odds	chances
offspring	children
oft	often
opportunity	a chance
oppose	to go against
oppress	to treat someone unfairly
orator	a public speaker
ornaments	jewellery
orphan	a child whose father passes away before he reaches maturity
outskirt	on the outside of a town
overrated	to give something more credit than it deserves

Pp

pangs	sharp pains
partake	to take part of
passage	a way through

patience	not getting angry or upset during suffering
peak	at the top of
perceive	to realize
perish	to be destroyed
persevere	to stay steadfast and strong on a course of action
pilgrim	one who is on a holy journey
pity	to feel sorry for someone
plead	to ask imploringly
plot	plan, a piece of land
ponder	to think about
portent	a sign of something which is to happen
portion	a piece of something
possess	to have as one's own, to take in control
preach	to teach publicly
precinct	an area
prefer	to like something more than something else
preserve	to maintain something in its original condition
prevent	to put a stop to something
pride	to be pleased with oneself
proclaim	announce publicly
procure	to get something
profit	a monetary gain
proposal	an offer put forwards, also used for when one asks someone for their hand in marriage
prostration	to bow on the floor with the head, feet, hands and knees touching the ground
protection	to look after someone making sure they are not harmed
pyre	a large pile of wood upon which a dead person is burnt

Qq

quarrel	fight
quench	to put an end to ones thirst

Rr

ram	a male sheep
rebuke	to tell of by showing ones disapproval
recall	to remember

recompense	to pay back for something one has done wrong
reflect	ponder, think over
reform	to change for the better
refrain	to stay away from
refuge	to be in the state of safety from danger
reject	to turn something down
rejoice	show happiness
relate	narrate, to tell a story or incident
relief	aid, to find comfort from pain
remain	to stay
remnant	what remains
repay	to give back
repent	to express sorrow for past actions
reprimand	to tell off
reproach	to show disapproval of past actions
request	to ask
reside	to live
resign	to give up
resolve	to find a solution to a problem
resort	to turn to a certain action to solve a problem
resurrect	to bring back to life after death
retort	to reply harshly
retribution	a punishment given which one feels the punished deserves
rowdy	noisy
rumour	gossip spread from person to person

Ss

sacked	robbed
sacred black stone	in Arabic 'al-hajr al-aswad'. A stone from heaven which is placed at one corner of the Ka'bah.
sacrifice	slaughtering an animal for Allah or to give ones possessions away to please Allah
salwa	food from heaven given to Banu Isra'eel when they were wandering in the desert
satiate	to satisfy
scarce	rare, no readily avaiable

scheme	a devised plot
scold	to harshly tell someone off
scorching	extremely hot
scorn	to show hatred and rejection
scripture	sacred writing
seclude	to go into privacy
seek	to look for
semblance	to look like
sense	felt
service	work
servitude	being a slave to someone, to do everything someone of power asks
sever	to cut off
severe	very great
shied	to shy away from
shoo	to shun
shun	to turn away, reject
siege	to surround a place one cannot break into in order to try and get them to surrender when supplies run out
sincere	being true in ones actions, not doing an action with pretence deceiving the onlooker
sneer	to laugh or smile at with contempt
snide	to say something with contempt
solution	answer
sought	looked for
spouse	husband or wife
spurn	to turn away, reject
station	guards
stern	serious
stow	pack, put away
strife	fight, bitter dispute over an issue
stubborn	not willing to change their mind even though they are in the wrong
subdue	bring under control
submit	to give into something

successor	an heir, inheritor, one who takes the position of someone after their death
sufficient	enough, plenty
summon	to call forward
supervise	observe someone doing something and direct them on how to do it
supplication	a prayer
support	to help, give ones assistance to
suspend	hang

Tt

tabernacle	the box which contains tranquillity and the things which the family of Moosa عليه السلام and Haroon عليه السلام left behind
Tawrat	Arabic for Torah, the holy book sent to Moosa عليه السلام (the Old Testament)
tend	care for
testify	to declare something to be the truth
threat	for one to say they intend to cause harm to another
threshold	doorway
thus	as a result
tidings	news (generally good news)
tolerate	to put up with
torment	to cause pain
tornado	strong rotating winds
trace	sign, mark, trail
tranquillity	peace, to be at ease
trial	a test, a gathering kept to decide whether someone is innocent or guilty
tribe	large extended family, clan
tribulation	a test which causes suffering
trust	to believe someone to be true and reliable
tyrant	a cruel ruler

Uu

Umrah	the lesser pilgrimage, in which one circles around the Ka'bah seven times, walks between the two mountains of Safa and Marwa seven times and shaves one's head
unite	to get together for a common purpose

unity	being united, living together without any fighting
unjust	unfair
unnatural	against the norm
upper-hand	being in a better position, having an advantage

Vv

vain	for one to feel greatly important, thinking greatly of one's self
vegetation	plants and trees
vice	evil, sin
vicegerent	a deputy, someone left in charge to deal with important matters
vied	to compete
vow	promise

Ww

waver	to be unsteady
whim	a change of mind to go with something which one would not normally do
wilderness	in the wild
will	the document which states how ones possessions should be distributed after their death
willingness	to happily do something
withdrew	to take out or fall back
withhold	to hold back
wittingly	cleverly, slyly
wrath	extremely angry
wretched	very bad

Yy

Yajuj Majuj	Arabic for Gog Magog, the tribes imprisoned behind the iron wall by Zhul Qarnayn

Zz

Zaboor	Arabic for Psalms, the book revealed to Dawood ﷵ
Zakah	charity, the one fortieth which a Muslim takes out of his wealth and gives to the needy
zeal	eager, enthusiastic

Endnotes

Adam عَلَيْهِ السَّلَام

1 The angels realised that Adam عَلَيْهِ السَّلَام had been taught by Allah سُبْحَانَهُ and had been given the ability to acquire knowledge, whilst they only knew that which had been taught to them. This capacity to learn was his noblest quality. His knowledge encompassed that of recognising Allah as well as knowledge required to successfully inhabit the earth.

2 Adam عَلَيْهِ السَّلَام said, "السلام عليكم," to which the angels replied, "وعليك السلام ورحمة الله."

3 Adam عَلَيْهِ السَّلَام was given the privilege to dwell in Paradise however he wandered in it alone. One day when he woke up from his slumber he found a woman sitting by him. It was Hawwa رَضِيَ اللهُ عَنْهَا, Allah had created her from Adam's عَلَيْهِ السَّلَام lower left rib. She was to be his wife, a companion to give him comfort, solace and company.

4 Recall what Allah told the angels about placing a vicegerent on the earth. It was Adam's عَلَيْهِ السَّلَام fate that he would eat from the tree and consequently be sent down to the earth.

The First Murder

5 The children of Adam عَلَيْهِ السَّلَام and Hawwa رَضِيَ اللهُ عَنْهَا were born in pairs, one male and female. The male from one birth would get married to a female from another birth and vice versa. Qabil's twin sister was more beautiful than the twin sister of Habil. Qabil was not happy with the idea that Habil was going to marry his more beautiful twin sister.

6 In the previous nations when a sacrifice was offered to Allah, a fire would descend from the heavens and consume the sacrifice to show its acceptance. Allah showed that he had accepted Habil's offering so the decision should be made in his favour, Habil would marry Qabil's twin sister.

Sheeth عَلَيْهِ السَّلَام

7 Allah revealed four books and one hundred scrolls, which were small scriptures. The four books were the Tawrat (Torah) which was revealed to Moosa عَلَيْهِ السَّلَام, the Zaboor (Psalms) which was revealed to Dawood عَلَيْهِ السَّلَام, the Injeel (Gospel) which was revealed to Isa عَلَيْهِ السَّلَام and the Qur'an which was revealed to the Messenger Muhammad صَلَّى اللهُ عَلَيْهِ وَسَلَّم.

Allah also revealed one hundred and four scrolls, which in Arabic are known as 'Sahifah'. Sheeth عَلَيْهِ السَّلَام received fifty of these one hundred and four sahifah.

Idrees عليه السلام

8 The story mentioned is an Isra'eeli narration. An Isra'eeli narration is a narration from the previous books. As the original text of the Torah, Psalms and Gospel has been tampered with we do not know whether these narrations are true or false. So the ruling with regards to these narrations is that we neither believe them nor do we deny them.

9 Allah told Idrees عليه السلام that whatever good deeds anyone does will be written in his account. For this reason he wanted a longer life in order to accumulate good deeds in his account.

10 Allah had told the Angel of Death to take his soul out on the fourth heaven. The Angel of Death was surprised at this as he wondered how to get Idrees عليه السلام to the fourth heaven. On his way down from the heavens he came across Idrees عليه السلام on the fourth heaven. The Angel of Death took out his soul here as Allah commanded.

Nooh عليه السلام

11 Wadd, Suwa, Yaguth, Ya'ooq and Nasr were pious predecessors. The people made statues of them after their deaths in remembrance of them. Shaytaan then convinced them to worship these idols.

12 He called his people towards the oneness of Allah for 950 years.

13 They would mock Nooh عليه السلام saying what use is an ark so far inland.

14 " وفارالتنور " – "And the ovens burst." (Quraan 11:40). In those days the ovens were holes dug in the ground with fire in them. So water started gushing out of places that contain fire.

15 Nooh عليه السلام had four children. Haam, Saam and Yafith were believers. This is a reference to his fourth son, Qan'aan.

16 Nooh عليه السلام had prayed to Allah to save his family and the believers. When he saw his son drown he asked Allah why he had not saved that member of his family. Allah reprimanded him for asking that question and stated that this son was not from amongst his family as Qan'aan was a polytheist. The word 'family' had implied those who believed. The question Nooh عليه السلام posed was due to a misunderstanding.

17 It is said that only children were born from the children of Nooh عليه السلام. None of the other surviving believers had children of their own. So according to this all people who came after Nooh عليه السلام their lineage goes back to him. This is why he

is known as the second Adam.

Salih 🕮

¹⁸ When they were asked what kind of miracle they want to see the people of Thamud asked for a child-bearing red camel to be brought forth from the mountain.

¹⁹ It was decided that the she-camel and their animals would have turns in drinking from the well. One day would be for the she-camel and one day for their animals.

²⁰ The she-camel is referred to as 'a sign from Allah' in the Quraan.

²¹ Qidar bin Salif along with eight of his men planned to kill the she-camel. They lay in ambush waiting by the well.

²² The nine men made a plan to strike Salih 🕮 all at once. By doing this they would not be able to exact the one who delivered the fatal blow. As they would not be able to identify which one of them killed him they would all be able to say that they did not do it. (Though they were planning on killing a messenger of Allah, observe how they made sure they avoided lying. Now ponder over how easily we tell lies.)

Ibrahim 🕮

²³ Ibrahim 🕮 was trying to show the people that the sun, moon and stars cannot be gods. They rise and set with the command of Allah, they have no control over when they rise, how long they shine or when they set. If they are unable to control their own path then how can they control, benefit or harm the lives of man? Allah is the one true god who is always there and his existence is not dependant on anyone or anything.

²⁴ Though outwardly this seems like a lie, Ibrahim 🕮 did not in fact lie. Allah has called him by Siddeeq in the Qur'an, attesting to his honesty and truthfulness. Ibrahim meant one thing by this and the people understood something else.

²⁵ Again this is not a lie, Ibrahim is using rhetoric to make the people understand. Ibrahim had previously shown the people the sun moon and stars have no power over themselves let alone being able to affect the lives of others. However they failed to understand such simple reasoning. So Ibrahim promised to plan against their idols. Now that he had broken them and had left the largest one he wanted the people to see the uselessness and stupidity of worshipping idols. They cannot benefit or harm, they are unable to protect themselves never mind other people. Now that only the largest was left he told them to ask it whether it had broken all the other idols, or maybe he might have seen who did it. The people realised that the idols cannot do anything,

they realised the truth in Ibrahim's words but refused to let go.

26 It is said that the fire was so hot that the people were unable to approach it. They could not fathom out how to get Ibrahim إِلَيْهِ into the fire. Shaytaan gave them the idea of a catapult. A catapult was built and was used to throw Ibrahim إِلَيْهِ into the fire.

27 This was a very clever challenge that Ibrahim إِلَيْهِ proposed. The king did not reply to this challenge because he knew that if he claimed to make the sun rise from the east and told Ibrahim إِلَيْهِ to tell his Lord to make it rise from the west then Allah would have done so and he would have lost his claim to divinity. (*See introduction for a detailed explanation.*)

28 Ibrahim إِلَيْهِ told the King that Saarah رَضِيَ was his sister because if he told him that she was his wife then the king would have had him killed in order to take her as his own. It was not a lie when he stated that she was his sister because he was implying they were brother and sister in faith.

29 Ibrahim إِلَيْهِ had been longing for a child for a long time. When the opportunity came for him to have another wife he married Haajira رَضِيَ. He was overjoyed that a child was born to him. Allah wanted to test him to see who he loved more, Allah or his new-born son. So Allah commanded him to leave his wife and son alone in a barren desert. Allah had also commanded him not to speak to them.

30 After he had killed the four birds he was told to mix up their parts and put them on four different hills.

Isma'eel عَلَيْهِ

31 Muslims still imitate this action of Hajaar رَضِيَ whenever they go for Umrah or Hajj.

32 Some narrations say that Jibra'eel عَلَيْهِ came and struck the ground, from there the water of Zamzam gushed out. Some say that Zamzam gushed from the place where Isma'eel عَلَيْهِ scraped his heel.

33 The bird they saw stays near water. The tribe of Jurhum had passed through that valley many times and did not know of any water source nearby. So they decided to investigate.

34 Ibrahim إِلَيْهِ had prayed to Allah to make the hearts of some people yearn for it.

35 This action too is imitated in hajj. Some narrations state that Shaytaan went to Ibrahim عَلَيْهِ on all three occasions.

36 It is said that Isma`eel told his father to turn him face down as this would ensure he does not see his face whilst carrying out Allah's command. Isma'eel ﷺ, though still a young child, feared that his father would be moved if he was to look upon his face and would not have carried out Allah's command. Observe how eager Isma'eel ﷺ was in making sure his father fulfils Allah's command even though this way of severing his head would not have brought about instant death and would have prolonged his agony.

37 Ibrahim ﷺ was residing in Sham with Saarah ﷞.

38 In the past when people went hunting they would travel long distances in search of game. As Isma'eel ﷺ would have been gone for a long period of time Ibrahim ﷺ returned home.

39 The Ka'bah had been built previously by Adam ﷺ. The Ka'bah was destroyed by the flood that drowned the disbelieving people of Nooh ﷺ. However the foundations remained hidden, buried under the sand. Allah commanded Ibrahim ﷺ to raise the Ka'bah on these foundations.

40 This white stone is known in Arabic as 'Hajar ul-Aswad', which translates as 'the Black Stone'. It has been narrated that whosoever kisses the black stone their sins will be forgiven. As more and more people did this, gradually the white stone became darker and darker until it has become the Black Stone.

41 This stone is found at the Station of Ibrahim ﷺ (Maqam Ibrahim ﷺ), near the Ka'bah. It has imprinted in it the footprints of Ibrahim ﷺ.

42 This was an indication towards people coming from near and far to do the pilgrimage. Though there was nobody around to hear his proclamation for Hajj, people would come on foot, which means they live close by, and people would come from far, on camels which had become lean due to the length of the journey.

Lut ﷺ

43 Ibrahim ﷺ is known as 'Kahlil ul-lah', which means the friend of Allah. Lut ﷺ was Ibrahim's ﷺ nephew.

44 They would refrain from the evil acts that their people used to commit.

45 These were the three angels who came to visit Ibrahim ﷺ to give him glad tidings about the birth of his son, Is'haaq ﷺ. Lut ﷺ knew the character of his town-folk, so he feared his people would harm the three guests because of their youthful appearances and good looks.

46 This was their final test to see if they desist from their evil ways when Lut عليه السلام tells them to leave his guests alone.

47 Lut عليه السلام was unaware that his three guests were angels, so he feared for them and prayed for refuge in a mighty power.

48 The wife of Lut عليه السلام used to side with the town-folk.

Is'haaq عليه السلام

49 Ibrahim عليه السلام was famous for his hosting. Despite the fact that there were only three guests he had a whole calf roasted for them.

50 Ibrahim عليه السلام thought they were shy, so he started to eat thinking they would join him.

51 When the angels had given Ibrahim عليه السلام and Saraah عليها السلام the glad tidings of a child, Is'haaq عليه السلام, they also gave tidings of a grandson from Is'haaq عليه السلام, who would be Ya'qub عليه السلام.

Ya'qub عليه السلام

52 When the angels gave the glad tidings of Is'haaq عليه السلام to Ibrahim عليه السلام and Saarah عليها السلام they also gave them the news of a grandchild, Ya'qub عليه السلام.

Yusuf عليه السلام

53 Ya'qub عليه السلام realised this dream meant that Yusuf عليه السلام would be granted apostleship and a high status. As his other sons were already jealous of Yusuf عليه السلام he told him not to relate the dream to them in case they understand it and intend to cause him harm.

54 They needed to corroborate their story with evidence so that their father would believe it. They decided to slaughter a ram and cover Yusuf's عليه السلام clothing with its blood. They would then claim that a wolf ate him.

55 They told Yusuf عليه السلام to look after their goods whilst they raced one another. They were trying to say that as we were far away from Yusuf عليه السلام we did not know his situation and were unable to come to his aid.

56 The brothers presented the blood stained shirt and claimed that a wolf ate him. Ya'qub عليه السلام knew they were lying because the shirt was not torn from anywhere. If a wolf had attacked him then it would have torn Yusuf's عليه السلام shirt as he struggled to fight it off.

⁵⁷ Whilst Yusuf ﷺ was alone in the dark well he was informed by Allah that he would remind his brothers of what they had done to him while they are unaware of his identity.

⁵⁸ When the man dropped the bucket into the well Yusuf ﷺ held on to it and was drawn out of the well.

⁵⁹ They hid Yusuf ﷺ away in order to sell him on as a slave.

⁶⁰ The minister's wife was drawn towards Yusuf's ﷺ beauty.

⁶¹ Yusuf ﷺ tried to get away. When he finally managed to open the locked door the minster was stood there. Upon seeing her husband, to avoid getting into trouble, the minister's wife quickly responded to the situation by blaming Yusuf ﷺ for making an advance on her.

⁶² Yusuf ﷺ denied the accusation of the minister's wife claiming she was the one who made an advance on him. So a person of the household who was present said that if Yusuf's ﷺ shirt is torn from the front then the minister's wife is a truthful and Yusuf ﷺ is a liar. He made this judgement upon the fact that if Yusuf ﷺ was making the advance towards her then she would have spurned him by pushing him from the front which would have caused Yusuf's ﷺ shirt to rip from the front. If it was ripped from the back then she is a liar and Yusuf ﷺ is truthful because it implied that Yusuf ﷺ was trying to get away and she grabbed his shirt from the back causing it to tear.

⁶³ As the shirt was found to be torn from the back they realised Yusuf ﷺ was truthful.

⁶⁴ The minister's wife was unable to tolerate the comments people were making regarding her love for her slave. In order to ridicule the women who had mocked her she held a banquet for them, in which she planned that they too would be mocked.

⁶⁵ The minister's wife called Yusuf ﷺ whilst they were busy cutting their food with their knives. When they saw Yusuf ﷺ they were taken aback by his outstanding beauty. The women continued to gaze at him not realising they were still cutting their food. They were captivated by his beauty to such an extent that they cut their hands. Either they did not notice they had cut their hands or they were trying to show Yusuf ﷺ that they were so entranced by his beauty they lost their senses and were cutting their hands without realising it.

⁶⁶ The minister's wife had achieved her aim to ridicule the women, that they had been so captivated by Yusuf's ﷺ beauty they cut their hands. Now that the women had seen the beauty of Yusuf ﷺ and realising she would no longer be

ridiculed for her evil intentions she openly confessed her desire.

67 When the minister saw his wife's infatuation for Yusuf ﷺ he decided to jail him until the matter died down.

68 Before he told them the interpretation of the dream he invited them towards the oneness of Allah. To ensure that the prisoners do not become restless as to when he would give the interpretation and so that they listen attentively he told them he would tell them the interpretation before their meal is brought to them.

69 Either Shaytaan made the man forget to mention that Yusuf ﷺ, an innocent man, had been thrown into prison or Shaytaan made Yusuf ﷺ forget to put his reliance in Allah. Though there is no sin in asking assistance from fellow men some deeds do not behove the messengers and the pious. It did not behove someone of Yusuf's ﷺ calibre and high rank that along with having complete trust in Allah he should also depend on any other means.

70 The prisoner regarding whom Yusuf ﷺ had said he would press wine for the king.

71 In order to establish his honesty, trustworthiness and the fact that he had not deceived his master in his absence he asked the king to investigate the truth behind his imprisonment. He wanted to be proved innocent so that he can later be placed in a position of trust. If his integrity was not proven at this point there was the possibility of people slandering him after he had been freed from jail.

72 According to the interpretation of the dream, the harvest was sown for seven years. They took out what was required and would store the rest of it away. In this manner they were able to amass a considerable amount over the years. When the famine arrived those afflicted were driven to Egypt for food as Egypt had large reserves stored.

73 Yusuf ﷺ having had his honesty and trustworthiness established was appointed over the storehouses. When the brothers came to Egypt in search of food they were directed to Yusuf ﷺ. Yusuf ﷺ recognised them but after so many years and expecting Yusuf ﷺ to have died a long time ago they did not recognise him.

74 Yusuf ﷺ and Binyamin had the same mother whilst the other sons of Ya'qub ﷺ had different mothers. Ya'qub ﷺ had greater love for Yusuf ﷺ and Binyamin. Binyamin had not been involved in the plans of the brothers. Yusuf ﷺ wanted to be reunited with his beloved brother, Binyamin, so in order to ensure the brothers return to Egypt he hid the goods with which they had used to pay for the food in their sacks.

75 How Ya'qub ﷺ was unwilling to part from Yusuf ﷺ, similarly he feared separation from Binyamin.

76 When the food ran out Ya'qub ﷺ knew that they would not receive any more from the Azeez of Egypt so he was compelled to send his son Binyamin.

77 When Yusuf ﷺ saw Binyamin he was overwhelmed, in privacy he informed him of who he was.

78 Yusuf ﷺ needed to devise a plane which would allow him keep his brother Binyamin with him without arousing any suspicion from his brothers. The Egyptian law did not allow him to detain a foreigner, so he planned to have him kept behind for stealing the king's measuring bowl.

79 Yusuf ﷺ knew the laws of Can'aan having spent his childhood there. It stated that the person who steals is detained and given in lieu to the person he had stolen from. So they asked the brothers what the punishment should be if one of them is found to be the thief. The brothers said they would pass judgement according to the law of their land, which allowed the person from whom the item was stolen to keep the thief. They were unaware that the bowl was in Binyamin's sack.

80 When they saw that Binyamin had the bowl they made an accusation against their long lost brother, Yusuf ﷺ, that he must have also been a thief.

81 The brothers remembered the oath they had taken with their father, they would bring Binyamin back. So they asked Yusuf ﷺ to take one of them in Binyamin's place. Yusuf ﷺ sought Allah's protection from doing such a thing as they had agreed that they would deal according to the law of their homeland. Like this Allah made it such that Yusuf ﷺ was able to be reunited with his brother after years of separation.

82 Ya'qub ﷺ said this after the remaining brothers went home and had told Ya'qub ﷺ what the eldest brother had told them to say.

83 Now three sons were absent, Yusuf ﷺ, Binyamin and the eldest one.

84 The brothers were startled that the Azeez had mentioned their long lost brother. When they looked carefully at his features they were able to discern the face of Yusuf ﷺ and thus asked him if he was Yusuf ﷺ.

85 The dream that Yusuf ﷺ had seen when he was a child, which mentioned at the beginning of the narrative, had finally come true.

Shu'ayb السلام

86 Shu'ayb السلام is known as the 'Orator of Messengers'.

87 They said they would have killed Shu'ayb السلام if they did not fear the retribution from his family. So Shu'ayb السلام asked them, 'Do you fear my family more than you fear Allah?'

88 He had lost all hope that anyone else from his people would bring faith.

Ayyoub السلام

89 Along with all the blessings Allah had given him he lost his children, wealth and health.

90 The illness and state of Ayyoub السلام became unbearable to the people and they could no longer tolerate him living in close proximity to them.

91 Some say that she sold her braids to earn for her livelihood. She had been driven to do this as people would not allow her to work for them fearing that Ayyoub's السلام illness will spread to them through her presence amongst them. Some say she asked for medicine from a person posing as a doctor not realising that it was Shaytaan. Ayyoub السلام ascertained that he was Shaytaan when the man was described to him. So he made an oath to lash her if he was to recover from his illness.

92 Ayyoub السلام was in a predicament. He had taken an oath to lash his wife a hundred times due to displeasing him. Now that he had regained his health and was able to carry out the deed he was faced with a dilemma. On the one hand he was gentle and humble so he could not hurt his wife. On the other hand he was patient and constant so he could not break the oath. Allah inspired him to take a hundred blades of grass and strike her with them. Like this he was able to fulfil his oath without causing his wife any harm.

93 Ayyoub السلام was very wealthy so Allah asked him if he had not been given enough already. To this Ayyoub السلام replied that though he had been given much he would never be independent of Allah's blessings.

Yunus ibn Matta السلام

94 Yunus السلام had left the town when he saw that the punishment of Allah was imminent. However he had not yet been commanded by Allah to leave. Though the signs indicated that the people were going to be destroyed it did not behove a messenger to leave without the command of Allah.

95 They drew lots to decide which person should be thrown off the ship. It is

also said that the people believed that when there was a storm it was due to a runaway slave being aboard the ship. In order to subdue the storm the slave had to be thrown overboard.

Moosa عليه السلام and Haroon عليه السلام

96 Banu Isra'eel were descendants of Ya'qub عليه السلام and his sons.

97 Moosa's عليه السلام mother put him in a box and placed the box in the river. The current took the box towards Firown's palace.

98 Firown was childless. Allah put love for him in the heart of Firown's wife and immediately she wanted to take him in as their own.

99 Moosa عليه السلام would not feed from any of the women that were present so more women were called. He refused every single one. When Moosa's عليه السلام sister saw this she approached them and told them of a woman that the baby would not reject. She did not disclose to them that she was the mother of the child. So Moosa's عليه السلام mother was sent for. In this manner Allah returned her child back to her as he had promised.

100 Moosa عليه السلام rebuked the Isra'eeli for being quarrelsome. The Isra'eeli misunderstood his rebuke and thought that Moosa عليه السلام was coming to strike him whereas he was really going to break up the fight.

101 When the Isra'eeli said this the Copt understood that Moosa عليه السلام was the one who killed the man the previous day. He ran to the court of Firown to inform him of this.

102 A man who was partial to Moosa عليه السلام went and told him of the order to arrest him.

103 They had to wait till the end to water their flock as the other men were bigger and stronger. They explained that their father was old and was unable to water the flock.

104 He related to the old man the situation that had befallen him and how he was forced to flee.

105 The daughter had observed that Moosa was عليه السلام strong as he had lifted the cover of the well by himself when usually several men were needed to lift it off. Furthermore Moosa عليه السلام was honest and modest as he made sure to walk in front of the daughter, who directed him from behind, whilst they were travelling to their house.

106 Allah is the all-Knowing. He asked Moosa عليه السلام regarding what was in his hand

in order to ensure that Moosa ﷺ could acknowledge that he was indeed holding his staff. As the night was dark Moosa ﷺ could have possibly thought that he had accidently picked up a snake instead of his staff when he saw the running snake, resulting in the confusion of Moosa ﷺ regarding the miracle.

107 When Firown saw that the magicians he had hired to defeat Moosa ﷺ had submitted to him he was greatly angered. He accused the magicians of conspiring with Moosa ﷺ before the contest. To avoid losing his power and hold over the people he indicted them of planning to lose to him. He alleged that Moosa ﷺ was their teacher who had taught them magic and that they had planned all this beforehand.

108 When the famine became unbearable they went to Moosa ﷺ and asked him to pray to his Lord to remove their affliction. They promised to change their ways. So Moosa ﷺ prayed and the punishment was uplifted. But the people were untrue to their word, so Allah sent a flood. Again when this became unbearable they went to Moosa ﷺ and made the same promise. They continued in this manner as the punishments came one after the other.

109 This was food sent down from heaven.

The Quest for Knowledge

110 In terms of the knowledge that comes with apostleship, Moosa ﷺ was the most knowledgeable person of the time.

111 This person had been given a different branch of knowledge which Moosa ﷺ had not been taught.

112 When Moosa ﷺ learnt of the more knowledgeable person he wanted to go and learn from him. Reflect on the humility of Moosa ﷺ. After being reprimanded by Allah and being told that there was a more knowledgeable person than him he did not became envious nor did he harbour any ill will towards the person. Rather he wanted to put himself at the service of that person to acquire knowledge from him. If we were put in a similar situation wherein we mentioned our great prowess in a certain field, then someone was to object and say there is someone who is more advanced than us in that field, how would we react?

113 He killed the child because he was going to grow up to be disobedient and would have led his parents astray from the true religion. Allah blessed them with another child who was pious and obedient.

114 Before passing away the parents of the two orphans had hidden wealth for them under a wall. Over time the wall had started to crumble and was close to collapsing. This would have exposed their wealth to others. The children were

still young. They would not have been able to defend themselves and their inheritance might have been stolen from them.

115 As Moosa's ﷺ quest was for knowledge, Khidr ﷺ gave him an example of how much knowledge they had compared to that of Allah's. The sip of water that the sparrow took does not compare to the vast ocean. Khidr ﷺ was only giving an example; Allah's knowledge did not decrease by granting them knowledge. Allah's knowledge can never decrease as Allah is al-A'leem. This name means that Allah's knowledge has reached the height of perfection and he has knowledge of everything, thus Allah's knowledge does not decrease. Nor does it increase as he already knows everything.

The Murder in Banu Isra'eel

116 The people asked for a description of the cow. Had they slaughtered any cow and done what was asked, it would have been sufficient and Allah's command would have been fulfilled. Banu Isra'eel foolishly continued asking questions regarding the cow making it difficult on themselves to find a cow of that description.

An Encounter with Death

117 It has been narrated that messengers are asked if they want to die when their time comes. The Angel of Death forgot to ask Moosa ﷺ, which angered him. This is the reason why he hit the Angel of Death.

118 Moosa ﷺ was told to place his hand on the back of a bull. For every hair that comes under his hand Allah would give Moosa ﷺ an extra year to live.

Yusha ﷺ

119 They were supposed to say 'Hittah', which means repentance, but due to their arrogance they changed the words to 'Habbah', which means wheat.

Shamuil ﷺ

120 Their number was three hundred and thirteen

Dawood ﷺ

121 He had passed judgement without listening to the other brother.

122 This incident occurred after Adam ﷺ had been created.

123 As there was no way of discerning who the mother of the child was, Dawood عليه السلام relied on the maturity and seniority of the elder woman. Furthermore the older woman was in possession of the child and the younger woman could not procure any evidence to prove it was her child. However, Sulayman عليه السلام had thought of an alternative way of establishing who the mother was. He wanted to see the reaction of the women if the child was ordered to be halved. When the command was given, the true mother of the child would not be able to bear to see her child killed. The older woman remained silent whereas the younger woman became restless and insisted the child be handed to the other woman, whole and unharmed. Her reaction was testimony to the fact that she was the mother as she could not see her child come to harm.

124 The value of the crops that the sheep had eaten totalled the value of the sheep. Hence Dawood عليه السلام gave the sheep in lieu of the crops. However Sulayman عليه السلام felt that by doing so the owner of the sheep would lose his means of a livelihood. He therefore set him to work on the field of the farmer to till the crops until they grew to their original state, whilst the farmer would keep the sheep, making use of its wool and milk.

125 Abu Hurayrah رضى الله عنه narrates from Rasulullah صلى الله عليه وسلم that he said, Sulayman عليه السلام the son of Dawood عليه السلام said, 'Tonight I will go to each of my seventy wives so that she may give birth to a knight who will fight in the path of Allah.' His companion said, 'In sha Allah,' but Sulayman عليه السلام did not repeat the words. As a result none of his wives conceived except one who gave birth to a child that had one part of its body missing." The Messenger صلى الله عليه وسلم added, "If he had said 'In sha Allah,' (if Allah wills) each one would have given birth to a child that would have strove out in the path of Allah."

126 In the verses of the Quraan we are not told to what test Sulayman عليه السلام had been subjected.

127 Sulayman عليه السلام was a great architect. In order to build great buildings with strong foundations he used the molten copper that Allah had caused to flow for him.

128 A Hoopoe is a type of bird, it was in the army of Sulayman عليه السلام.

129 The Queen reasoned with her ministers, saying that when kings conquer a place they destroy it and dishonour its respectable citizens. In order to avoid this and measure up Sulayman's عليه السلام might she sent some gifts to him.

130 It has been narrated that there is one name of Allah, known as the 'ism ul-A'zam'. If anyone was to pray to Allah taking this name then his prayer will definitely be accepted.

131 The reason why Sulayman ﷺ showed her the glass floor and had her throne changed was to see whether she would recognise the truth. Sulayman ﷺ gave her metaphorical examples of the foolishness of worshipping the sun. Their philosophy was that all good and evil belonged to the stars and since the sun was the biggest that was their god. They saw the benefits that the sun provided without which all vegetation would die, so they assumed that it had power. Sulayman's ﷺ examples showed that though outwardly the glass floor looked like water and the throne did not look like hers the reality of it was different. Similarly how they saw that the sun was benefitting the earth, the reality of it is that the sun is under the authority of Allah and is a manifestation of His power. The sun can only harm and benefit according to the will of Allah.

132 The jinn were subjugated to Sulayman ﷺ. They would construct large buildings for him, however they were forbidden to look towards Sulayman ﷺ. If they glanced at him they would be destroyed. Sulayman ﷺ was leaning on his staff supervising the jinn when he passed away. The jinn who claimed they knew the unseen continued working unaware of Sulayman's ﷺ death. The staff Sulayman ﷺ was leaning on was gradually gnawed away by an insect due to which after a long time the staff fell. Sulayman ﷺ no longer had anything to support him so he fell too. When a jinn glanced back, it was not destroyed. Only then did they realise that Sulayman ﷺ had passed away. Allah disproved the Jinns' claim that they knew the unseen as they did not know Sulayman ﷺ had passed away, otherwise they would have stopped working.

Uzair ﷺ

133 This incident is mentioned in the Quraan in Surah Baqarah. However the person upon whom this incident befell is not mentioned. Some scholars are of the opinion that it was Uzair ﷺ, whilst some are of the opinion that it was Armaya ﷺ.

134 Jews claim that Uzair ﷺ is the son of God. It has been said that over time the Tawrat had been lost to the Jews and they had forgotten the scripture. When Uzair ﷺ was given life again after a hundred years he still knew the Tawrat, rather than taking this as a sign of the power of Allah they later attributed divinity to Uzair ﷺ, calling him the son of God.

Maryam ﷡

135 Hannah was the name of the wife of Imran.

136 A khadim is a person who has dedicated his service to a place or a person.

137 Allah gave Maryam ﷡ fruit that did not grow in that season nor was it

available elsewhere at that time of the year. Zakariyya ﷺ had reached old age and normally people of his age do not have children. But witnessing the power of Allah, who could give Maryam ﷺ fruits that don't grow at that time of the year, his eyes bore witness that Allah could also give him a child despite his old age.

Zakariyya ﷺ

138 Had Allah not brought Zakariyya ﷺ to life before, when he had also been nothing? Similarly Allah could bring to life a son for Zakariyya ﷺ.

139 He was unable to talk because the arrival of Yahya ﷺ was soon. So through signs he told the people what to do.

140 There are two different narrations regarding Zakariyya's death, the chain of both narrations are end at the same narrator. One relates the incident mentioned whereas the other mentions that Zakariyya ﷺ died a natural death.

Yahya ﷺ

141 There are differing narrations regarding the specifics of Yahya's ﷺ death. The woman with whom Herod was infatuated differs in some, whereas some say that he had divorced his wife thrice. According to the Tawrat law, Yahya ﷺ said he could not take her back unless she marries another man first, this angered Herod.

Isa ﷺ

142 It is imperative to teach our children the true fundamental Islamic beliefs. A Muslim can come out of the fold of Islam if his beliefs are not in accordance to the Quraan and Sunnah. To have a belief contradicting that of the Quraan is very dangerous to a person's imaan. Children are taught different variations of the birth, life and death of Isa ﷺ. It is of paramount importance they can differentiate between truth and falsehood. For example it is stated in the Quraan that the pangs of birth drove Maryam ﷺ under a tree, she did not give birth to Isa ﷺ in a stable. There were no three wise men with gifts or shepherds. Furthermore some people think that a man named Joseph was the father of Isa ﷺ. Isa ﷺ had no father which is why his lineage in the Quraan is attributed to his mother, Isa ﷺ ibn Maryam ﷺ. The fact that Isa ﷺ has no father is the miracle that Allah wanted to show the people that Allah is not bound by means.

143 Reflect on the first words spoken by Isa ﷺ, 'I am the servant of Allah'. Allah made his first words a refutation of what people would later attribute, that Isa

ﷺ is the son of god. (May Allah protect us)

144 Ahmad ﷺ is another name of Muhammad ﷺ.

145 Hawariyyeen is the name given to the disciples of Isa ﷺ.

146 Isa ﷺ was raised to the heavens and the man who they had sent into the house to look for Isa ﷺ was made to look like Isa ﷺ. When the soldiers became concerned about the delay they entered the house and arrested the man who they had sent inside as he looked like Isa ﷺ.

147 The coming of Dajjal will be a great test for Muslims. He will first claim apostleship then he will claim to be god. He will be able to do many extraordinary feats which will mislead many Muslims into affirming what he claims.

148 Yajuj and Majuj are two destructive tribes. Zhul Qarnayn was a believer who is said to have ruled the known world. Once on an expedition he came across a pass between two mountains. A people resided here whose language was unfamiliar to him. They complained to him of the antics and trouble Yajuj and Majuj caused and offered to pay him to build a barrier between them and the Yajuj and Majuj tribes. Zhul Qarnayn offered to build the wall for free but asked for assistance from their people. He ordered them to collect iron pieces with which he erected an iron wall between the two mountains and strengthened it with molten copper. Yajuj and Majuj were unable to overcome the barrier nor were they able to break through. Close to Qiyamah they will suddenly appear and cause great turmoil in the land.

The Woman and the Dog

149 Allah forgave the woman for giving water to the thirsty dog despite all her evil deeds. He who has mercy on those on the earth then the One in the heavens will have mercy on him.

The Man who Feared Allah

150 The man thought that if he was burnt to ashes and his ashes were spread far and wide then Allah would be unable to raise him back to life. He feared Allah would deal severely with him due to his sins. However, Allah is all-powerful and is capable of doing anything without being limited by or restricted to any means. His power and might extend over all things. When the man was raised back to life, Allah forgave him because of his fear for Him.

Though my efforts are nothing, my efforts are meek,
It is only the priceless pleasure of my Lord that I seek.